WARRIGAL THE WARRIOR

This edition published 2017
By Living Book Press
147 Durren Rd, Jilliby, 2259
Copyright © The Estate of C.K. Thompson, 1948

Cover photo by Newretreads.

The publisher would like to give a huge 'Thank You' to the author's family
for their assistance in making this book available once more.

ISBN: 978-0-6481048-5-8

WARRIGAL THE WARRIOR

By C.K. Thompson, R.A.O.U., J.P.

(AUTHOR OF "KING OF THE RANGES," "MONARCH OF THE WESTERN SKIES," ETC.)

BY THE SAME AUTHOR

King of the Ranges
Old Bob's Birds
Maggie the Magnificent
Thunderbolt the Falcon
Monarch of the Western Skies
Wild Canary
Warrigal the Warrior
Blackie the Brumbie
Willy Wagtail
Red Emperor
Tiger Cat
Wombat

CONTENTS

Contents

DEDICATION.

To my old school and bush mate DOUGLAS PERRY, of Tenambit, N.S.W.

Dear Doug.,

It is a far cry to the old bush days when we were younger and the world, to our minds at least, was wider. Do you recall those happy times we spent with gun, rabbit trap, rod and reel, in country where the mournful howl of the hunting dingo has long since given way to civilisation and thriving settlement ? Particularly, do you remember that awful Christmas Day we spent helping to save the small settlement from the ravages of bush fire ? It is many years ago, but I still remember vividly that Black Christmas, and the frantic scenes as we fought desperately to save the homes of those good folk who, in between assisting us, piled their worldly goods into heaps in the sole street the little village possessed. There is not much bush there these days, and the village is a prosperous little town. I think it most fitting that you should now be Captain of the Tenambit Bush Fire Brigade, but my devout hope is that your equipment will get rusty through lack of use.

As a poultry farmer, you cannot be expected to love Warrigal; and it is rather anomalous that I should seek to immortalise him. My mind harks back to those days and nights—in East Maitland and Tenambit, over 20 years ago now, when the killer-dog made life miserable for poultry farmers.

After nine residents had lost fowls valued at hundreds of pounds, didn't you and I sit up, night after night, with rifles, awaiting the killer's onslaught upon my father's poultry run? And wasn't it positively maddening that when we decided to take a night off and get some sleep, on July 25, 1925, the killer struck, and my father lost 70 fowls, dragged one by one from their perches and left scattered all over the yard? They got him, but neither you nor I shared in the £20 reward.

I have some old newspaper cuttings telling of those days and nights when the killer stalked abroad, but it is all done with now.

Times change and the world marches on. I am reminded of those nostalgic lines of "Banjo" Paterson —

"I would fain go back to the old grey river,
To the old bush days when our hearts were
    light;
But, alas! those days they have fled for ever,
They are like the swans that have swept from
    sight.

And I know full well that the strangers' faces
Would meet us now in our dearest places;
For our day is dead and has left no traces
But the thoughts that live in my mind to-night."

There is a new generation that knows little about the bush and the creatures that inhabit it. I have not sought to glorify Warrigal, neither have I condemned him. I have just tried to present him as he really is, without fear or favour, affection or ill-will.

Warrigal is as Australian as are we human beings, and like us human beings, he is not all bad. He is as Nature fashioned him.

Yours for old time's sake,

—C. K. THOMPSON.

CHAPTER I.
THE HOME OF THE DINGO.

HIGH in the heavens the full moon rode in all her majestic splendor, shedding her soft radiance over the rugged mountain range. Around her glittered her uncounted starry companions, set in their dark velvet background as if some joyful sprite had thrown there with a prodigal hand a diamond shower in tribute to the Moon Queen.

The mountain range, under the glare of the noon day sun, showed ugly gashes where deep gorges, walled in by rugged, frowning crags and cliffs, cradled mountain creeks and silent pools; but the quiet lunar radiance softly painted this harshness into a canvas of wild beauty, hiding the ugliness and silvering the surf ace of the creeks and pools with leaf-filtered moonlight.

Out of the depths of a gorge came the mournful call of a tawny frogmouth, a quick run of echoing "ooms" which did nothing to relieve the loneliness. The mopoke kept up his monotonous call for a time and then, feeling hungry, left the limb of the tree on which he had been resting, and flew off, on muffled wings, in search of food.

On a huge, bare, domed rock which literally overhung the chasm, sat an old dingo like a stone idol. Sharp-etched

against the moon, his stiff ears erect and his bushy tail curled
slightly round his hind-quarters, he appeared to be waiting
for something to happen. Around him the mountains and
the bush were quiet. Not even the call of a mopoke, the
booming of a bittern or the harsh cry of a wandering curlew,
disturbed the peace. It was a rather ominous peace, as if
Nature were holding her breath in apprehensive expectation
of coming events that might not be pleasant.

Presently the old dingo unfroze. He turned his head this
way and that, but saw nothing to interest him. He looked
down over the edge of the rock into the chasm beneath
and saw less.

Raising his head and pointing his sharp muzzle to the
moon, he gave two yelps, paused, and then let out a long sad
howl as if the brooding silence were breaking his heart. Away
to the north came an answering howl, which was taken up
from near and far. It was as if the entire dingo population
had been awaiting the signal to commence.

The old dingo was a handsome dog, a purebred Warrigal whose ancient ancestors had roamed south-eastern
Asia when the world was very young. A silent and a deadly
hunter, his dark yellow body was just five feet long from the
end of his pointed muzzle to the tip of his bushy tail. His
short, stiff, pointed ears were always on the alert, and his
heavy jaws, distinctive for that terrible power that enabled
him to tear away completely the flesh gripped in their bite,
rarely missed their prey.

In this respect, however, he was not superior to any
member of the pack. Each and every dog was an experienced
hunter. Usually each hunted alone, or with his mate; only
when the game was too big for one or two to tackle did all
the wild dogs combine in the adventure.

For many years, the original pack, large in the seasons

when hunting was good, and small when game was not so plentiful, had hunted over prosperous territory in the far north as their ancestors had done before them. They had preyed upon all the marsupials, but chiefly the smaller kinds or the youngsters of the big kangaroos and wallaroos, and had found their living very good.

As time went on, however, hunting parties of white men began to slaughter the kangaroos and wallabies. Other men followed with their flocks of sheep and herds of fat cattle. The men wrought more destruction among the marsupials with guns and dogs and their flocks and herds with grass-hungry mouths. Poison set for rabbits had decimated the ground birds and had accounted also for many dingoes.

With their natural prey gone, the dingoes had to migrate to other country, but it was the same sorry story. No matter where they travelled, they found that men, eager to commercialise the skins of native animals, were depriving the wild dogs of their natural prey. In retaliation, and because they had to eat, the dingoes turned their attention to the sheep, lambs and calves of the human invaders.

Of course, the human settlers could not be expected to regard this with a friendly eye. They persecuted the dingoes ruthlessly with poison, trap and gun. Many men devoted the whole of their time to trapping and shooting dingoes. These men were called "doggers".

The pack to which the old dingo belonged had now established itself firmly among the rocky and precipitous gorges and bluffs of a mountain range which overlooked wide acres of grazing property. The various members lived in small caves, holes in the rocks, hollow logs and other shelters, rarely venturing out of their secure hiding places during the daylight hours; but as the sun went down, they began to emerge into the dusk, each on hunting business.

Like so many swift and silent shadows, they slipped down from their rocky fastnesses to the open plains, there to range far and wide.

In a small cave overlooking the edge of a rather steep cliff, the old dingo had established his home. His mate was not a true dingo.

Years before, a party of tourists from a distant city had spent a holiday on a sheep station. With them had been a very handsome collie. He was a venturesome dog who had been kept on a chain, but one beautiful warm night in early summer, he had managed to slip out of his collar and, exhilarated with a sense of freedom from restraint, had gone frisking and skipping around the paddocks, bent on an exploration by moonlight.

Down along the creek he had come face to face with a hunting female dingo. The surprise was mutual. The dingo had never seen such a dog before, and was very wary. As to the collie, he had seen nothing strange in the tawny dog. He had met all kinds of canines in his time, and this was just another one to him. Still feeling the exhilarating effects of his freedom, and a little intoxicated by the sweet cool air on the moonlit plains, his attitude was one of complete friendliness. He considered that nothing would be pleasanter than a romp with this newcomer.

His friendly overtures were not received kindly by the lady dingo. She had no desire to romp with the collie or with any other dog. She was hungry and was hunting for her evening meal. Thus, when the collie fawned upon her, she met him with rolled back lip and fierce white fangs, which abashed him. Still, he was ready to make concessions to a lady, so did not press his attentions upon her; but when she slid silently away among the trees, he trotted after her.

Nobody ever saw that handsome collie dog again. His

disappearance remained a complete mystery to the station owner and his city guests, who were forced to return home without their pet.

But, up in the hills where the dingoes lived, the collie and the lady dog he had met on the banks of the creek in the moonlight, became friends. The collie was not made very welcome by the rest of the pack. None of them liked him, and they were not backward in letting him know it. He stayed with them, leading an uneasy existence, for several weeks and fast tiring of the hostility and the hard life.

Life had been hard for him, too. He was no hunter. Before he had run away, food always had been provided for him by his master. He never had to worry where his next meal was coming from. In the dingo country it was different. Each animal had to fend for itself, and those that could not hunt had to go hungry. It is a fact that the collie would have died from starvation had not his dingo mate hunted for both of them.

The male dingoes resented his presence, one animal especially having no time for him. This was a hardy young dog who had long desired the female dingo for a mate. He was not a very courageous animal and did not feel like fighting for the lady; but he found ways and means of making life unpleasant for the poor collie.

Unable to stand the strain and the hard life any more, the collie resolved to return to the cattle station, and one day when the pack was sleeping in its various hide-outs, he slipped away, intent on making his way down from the hills and reaching the station with all possible speed.

Unfortunately, the collie was unused to these rugged places. He could not climb the rocks and slide down the slopes like the agile dingoes. So it transpired that, while attempting to negotiate a particularly treacherous piece of rocky ground, he missed his footing and fell hundreds of feet, to meet a lonely death at the bottom of the deep valley below.

Time passed, and his dingo mate became the mother of three little pups. One of these was carried off by a marauding wedge-tailed eagle; another, a sickly little animal, did not live. The third, however, a very handsome dog, something like her father, grew and thrived. In due course she mated with a member of the pack—the old dingo now sitting on the rock and serenading the moon.

Though there was as much collie as dingo in her, she was a good hunter and a good fighter, too, if the occasion demanded; but her ways were more gentle than those of her fierce fullblooded dingo sisters.

She had not gone out hunting this night, but had stayed at home in the cave with her young son, Warrigal. She was not feeling very well; in fact she had not felt well for several days, not since eating a dead rabbit she had found down a gorge leading out on to the plains.

So when her lord and master, the old dingo, had slipped out of their cave into the gathering dusk, she had not followed him. She felt quite confident that if the hunting was good, he would bring back something for Warrigal and her.

Squatting on his high rock and still howling dismally, the old dingo was trying to make up his mind whether he would prospect the plains in search of rabbits or small, sleeping ground birds, or try his luck after a lamb on a far distant sheep station. From many points around him came yelps and howls as if other members of the pack, too, were trying to make up their minds.

At last, becoming aware of the fact that a meal was most unlikely to jump up on the rock and into his mouth, the old dingo ceased howling, swung around on his haunches, dropped lightly to the ground and vanished into the thickets, presently to make his agile way down through the rocks and scrub until he reached the bottom of the gorge. He had no definite plans in mind, but was content to gather in anything that might present itself.

Luck was with him, because he had not gone far along the bottom of the gorge before he came to an open space. It was well grassed and was practically surrounded by stunted bushes. Right in the centre of the clearing was a large rabbit busily dining on the short grass, while another was doing likewise in the shadow thrown by a bush at the edge of the clearing.

The old dingo came to a halt and dropped into his characteristic crouch. Apart from the feeding rabbits, the bush around him was quiet. Without making the slightest sound, he began to creep to the right, seeking the cover of bushes and tufts of grass. Through these he crept, his tawny body pressed close to the earth, the rabbits quite unconscious of his presence—which was not surprising, for there is nothing more silent than the hunting dingo that sees the prey in its grasp.

His objective was the rabbit feeding near the bush, but before he could get to within leaping range, the furry animal moved out into the moonlight towards its companion. Quite undismayed, the old dog reached the bush and crawled under it. There he stayed for a few minutes, his body part of the shadows, his keen, fierce eyes boring into the rabbit's back.

With patience born of long experience, the dingo waited. The rabbit joined its companion and they fed together for a time. Then they separated, both making slow progress to the opposite side of the clearing.

The dingo cast searching eyes around the vicinity and what he saw satisfied him. Withdrawing backwards from the shelter of the bush, he began a swift, though silent, circuit, taking advantage of every piece of cover, merging his body with shadow where available, becoming part of a patch of sand when crossing a few yards of country devoid of any cover at all, and freezing into immobility when one of the rabbits sat up straight with quivering ears as though disturbed by some alien presence.

Quite satisfied in its own simple mind that all was well, the bunny again set to work on the tasty grass, and before it had moved three feet, the dingo was hidden under another bush exactly opposite the one under which it had first crouched.

As the feeding rabbit came nearer, the dingo shrank more and more into itself, tensing for the spring that would send it like a dart from a blowpipe at its prey.

Blissfully unconscious of impending disaster, the two rabbits, now feeding side by side again, came closer and closer to the bush.

His practised eye told the old dingo that the supreme moment had arrived. Like a yellow streak he flew through the air and, as he seized one rabbit in his terrible jaws, he hurled his body sideways, crushing the other down to earth. Swift bites deprived the first rabbit of its life and, dropping it, he quickly seized the second and it, too, died violently.

Certainly it had been a great stroke of luck for the old wild dog. Though hungry, he did not begin his meal on the spot. He had a marked dislike for open spaces.

Picking up one of the rabbits, he took it and dropped it behind a bush, and then returned for the other. This he also took behind a bush, and commenced to dine at his leisure.

His meal over, the old dingo picked up the second bunny in his mouth and began his homeward trek. Without allowing side issues to detract him, he went, as straight as geographical circumstances would permit, up the rugged rocky tracks that led him to his home cave. When he got there he deposited the rabbit at the feet of his mate and lay down at the entrance of the cave as she ate her meal.

Little Warrigal was dozing in the background, but instinct told him that food was handy. He became wide awake instantly and waddled forward for his share.

The old dingo did not do any more hunting that night. He paid a short visit to his favorite rock some hours before dawn, and exchanged a few companionable howls and yelps with a distant crony who was squatting on another rock overlooking another gorge. That, however, was a matter of habit.

As the sun peeped above the horizon, he retired to his cave where his wife and son were already sleeping.

CHAPTER II.
THE BIG ADVENTURE

By some mysterious means, some code of wild intelligence beyond the understanding of man, the rallying call for combined adventure had gone forth to the dingo pack.

There was big game on the plains. It was a task for the whole pack, and the members were gathering from far and near.

Squatting high up on his lookout rock, the old dingo's mournful hunting howl, tinged with menace, echoed and re-echoed among the forbidding ranges. Some pack members gave tongue in answer, but others did not trouble. They were not rallying in response to his yowling because they had received the message long before by some means known only to themselves.

As the moon rose higher and higher, its questing beams, filtering through the dense bushes and scrub, occasionally rested for a fleeting moment upon some tawny shape slipping silently to the rendezvous.

It was not until the last howl had died away, conveying to him the intelligence that every member of the pack was now either at the assembly point or on the way, that the old dingo descended from the rock to join his patient mate. Together they melted into the gloom and soon found themselves with the silent horde at the foot of the ranges.

In a compact mass, they moved across the plains, their objective a small mob of red kangaroos that had drifted in from the desert country farther out. It was not often that these big marsupials came so close to the foothills, but when they did, the dingoes considered it worth while to hunt as a pack—not only worth while, but safer. Full grown red kangaroos were too big for one or two wild dogs to tackle. It required the whole pack for that; for, should one be cornered he became a fighting fury. The dingoes knew that from past experience. Not a few of them had lost their lives trying to tackle kangaroos without adequate support. It was the custom of the whole pack to single out one big 'roo and, having run him down, to tackle him en masse and finish him off by sheer weight of numbers.

In prosperous days when the pack was large, the dingoes might separate into two, or even three, sections, each one pursuing and overcoming a big red marsupial.

High up among the rocks, little Warrigal, alone in the family cave, was feeling restless. He was fast nearing the age when his first serious lessons in hunting craft would be given him, and his savage little heart often beat faster in anticipation. He could not understand why his parents each night should slip away at dusk, leaving him alone, but they had impressed upon him in their own way that he was not to stir from the cave during their absence.

Warrigal had never been farther than the mouth of the cave in his life until this particular night. He was feeling very restless and unhappy. He wanted to be with his parents where ever they were. Though young, he, too, had received the mysterious message, though he did not fully understand its import. But he did realise that the occasion was an extra-special one. Something big was doing in the dingo world, bigger than anything that had ever happened before in his short life.

Why did they have to leave him out of it? He ambled around the small cave several times and then decided to take a very daring step. He made several false moves towards the mouth of the cave, but each time changed his mind about going outside, until, taking his courage in both paws, he stepped out into the moonlight.

For a moment he stood there breathless and undecided, casting about in his mind for an excuse to return inside the cave. He waddled forward a foot or two, and paused again. Nothing happened, and this emboldened him.

The mouth of the cave was only about six feet from the edge of the cliff, but Warrigal did not know this. It was, therefore, a very startled little dingo pup that, stepping forward confidently once more, found no further pebbles beneath his paws, and himself sliding rapidly downwards.

With a sharp yelp of fear, he tried to save himself, but, engulfed in a miniature avalanche of small stones and dirt, he went sliding and bumping towards the bottom of the valley.

It was fortunate for young Warrigal that the cliff, though high, was not a sheer drop, otherwise he would never have lived another minute. In the middle of a shower of pebbles and earth he finally shot over a three-foot drop and landed at the bottom of the ravine with all the wind, and most of the spirit of adventure, knocked out of him. He lay for a time among the stones, panting for breath, his small tongue hanging from his mouth.

All around him the ravine was silent, but this did not add to his discomfort because he was used to silence. It was part of his life, part of his ancestry. Far from scaring him, it actually gave him enough confidence to stand up on his stout little legs and take stock of his surroundings.

Presently he began to amble along the ravine bottom, finding the going fairly easy among the scrub and short tufted grass. Not knowing or caring where he was going, but with confidence increasing with every extra yard he covered, he proceeded towards the open country. Once he almost fell into a pool of water, but managed to save himself with a quick backward scramble. A wallaby hopping towards the water caused him brief disquiet, but it did not attempt to interfere with him and he was more than content not to seek an introduction to it.

After about an hour's ambling he had not gone very far, partly owing to the now patchy nature of the ground, but mostly because of his inquiring nature. He often turned aside to investigate strange objects, but none were of sufficient interest to hold his attention for long.

His exertions got the better of him before dawn, and when he found a small fissure beneath a rock, he crept into it and went to sleep. He was still asleep when the sun came up, but its hot rays, beating on the rock under which he lay, turned the shelter into a bush oven. The heat proving too much for him, he decided to move on, though he did not fancy travelling in broad daylight. He had never been out in it before. Still, he told himself, there always had to be a first time.

Following the ravine bottom, he eventually came to flatter country. Waddling steadily forward, his time very much his own, little Warrigal found himself on the edge of a wide open space occupied only by several small hills. He did not know that they were the nests of termites. In the long ago, trees had occupied this clearing. Then the termites, or white ants, had taken possession and now practically nothing remained of the former giants of the bush.

As he neared one of these nests, the pup became aware of a small animal industriously scratching a hole in the base of the mound. It was about a foot long, with a short bushy tail, and had white bands across its grey back.

Being busy, it did not notice the little dingo approaching. Inquisitive Warrigal, unafraid and with a desire to be friendly waddled to within a yard or two of the animal before it saw him. Sitting up, its bright little eyes regarded him with terror. Leaving the half-scratched hole, it ran, nimble-footed, across the open space to where a small burrow was just visible among the tufts of spindly grass. Before disappearing into it, the animal sat up and threw another startled glance at the interested Warrigal, who at once began to waddle across to it. That was sufficient for the little ant-eater. It dived straight into its burrow and vanished.

Warrigal felt a glowing sense of pride. That animal had been afraid of him! Though only a pup, he had in his veins the blood of a long line of hunting dogs, the majority of which preferred to meet a foe that was unwilling, or could not fight. So it was that Warrigal felt proud. Had he known that the animal was a numbat, or banded ant-eater, one of the shyest and most elusive creatures of the bush—quite harmless and defenceless, and no match for even a dingo pup—it would not have lessened that pride.

On the best of good terms with himself, Warrigal crossed the clearing and into the denser thickets beyond. As he was passing over a brief patch of sand, he got a surprise when he came face to face with a big frilled lizard that was sunning itself on the warm ground. The lizard looked at Warrigal and warrigal looked at it. The lizard had its big frill closely folded to its neck, but when the little dingo cringed back, it opened its jaws, raising its big frill, and hissed hoarsely.

Taken completely aback, Warrigal turned tail and bolted,

not knowing that the lizard was nothing but a big bluffer. Seeing him depart, the lizard dropped its frill and lay on the ground again. Warrigal came to a halt behind some bushes that hid the lizard from sight, and then peered cautiously round at the thing that had scared him. As the lizard made no move to molest him, he decided to go on, but as he wanted to cross the space where the lizard was, he was in a quandary.

He left the bush and waddled warily towards the ugly creature. The lizard saw him coming, but did not anticipate any aggression. Warrigal resolved to make a dash past it, trusting to his feet to get him out of danger, so made for it with a rush, intended to skirt it. The lizard saw him coming and, getting up, bolted for the shelter of a bush, its long tail held upwards and its neck-frill folded. Warrigal, without knowing it, had called the creature's bluff.

Observing the lizard scuttling away, Warrigal's pride knew no bounds. Two bush creatures had shown they were afraid of him. He was a pup to be respected and had he been a cat he would have purred.

On he went but nature began to catch up with him. He started to feel hungry and thirsty, but there was no food for him here, neither did he know how or where to find any. The heat of the sun at length forced him to take shelter under a saltbush, and here he dozed for several hours.

It was when the sun was slowly sinking towards the distant horizon that he decided to move on. By now he was desperately hungry and thirsty, and regretting from the bottom of his small heart that he had ventured from the family cave during the night. He staggered from under the saltbush with some vague idea of trying to retrace his steps to the ravine.

And then, as he waddled wearily away, his little ears

drooping and his small tail sagging to the ground, he met Adventure—Real Adventure—for, as he rounded a rock, he came across a huge creature, the like of which he had never conjured up in his wildest imaginings.

Charlie Harrison, gun under his arm and bag on his back, got quite as big a surprise as the small dingo pup. He gazed down on it in amazement, while the little dog looked up at him in equal astonishment.

"A dingo pup out here!" exclaimed the white man, involuntarily bringing his gun to the ready. "Now, how in the name of fortune did he get here?"

Little Warrigal sat back on his haunches and stared at the strange two-legged creature in amazement. He put his head on one side and then on the other as Harrison raised his gun and then lowered it. He watched with interest as the man reversed the weapon, taking the barrel in his hand.

As he quietly raised it with the intention of bringing the butt down with a smashing blow upon the small pup's head, Warrigal quite unaware of impending disaster, stood up and, waddling to the man's feet, sniffed at his boots. Harrison, the gun upraised, looked surprised. Then, when the small dog gave a sharp little yelp and gazed up at him with its head cocked on one side, he lowered the gun to his side.

"Cut it out, will you, pup, and give me a fair go," he said sternly. "I'm a dingo-killer. It is my job to wipe you out and your whole destructive family with you. This is no time to be friendly. We're enemies, you young villain. Dingoes and doggers do not chum up you know."

Warrigal was interested in hearing the man's voice, but he did not feel afraid of him. He had no cause to. He had never seen a man before, so how could he know that this creature was a deadly enemy?

Sinking down on his haunches and mentally reproaching

himself for being a fool, Harrison held out his hand and made coaxing noises to the pup. Warrigal sat on the ground and made no response, so the man leaned forward and deliberately tickled his furry throat. The pup shrank back a little, but did not run away, so, following up the advantage, the dogger patted it on the head, and then tickled its right ear.

When Warrigal put out a small tongue and licked his hand, Harrison was lost. Still squatting on his haunches he looked at the small dingo, which returned the compliment.

"This is a nice state of affairs, I must say," said the perplexed bushman. "I can't allow you to go free, my friend, and yet, how on earth can I kill you in cold blood? Take my advice, my little dingo mate, and run away. Go on, bolt for the mountains while your luck is in."

He made a menacing gesture at Warrigal, who merely looked interested. This strange creature apparently wanted to play games. Warrigal thought that a frolic with him would be nice; but he was really too hungry, too tired and too thirsty to play games.

"Well, if you won't go home to your mother, you won't, I guess," said the puzzled bushman. "However, that is your affair. I've got things to do, so I'll wish you good-bye. But I'm telling you this, my young Warrigal friend: you had better keep a wary eye out in the future. You won't always find me as soft-hearted as this! Cheerio, you little villain. Go home to your mother."

Getting to his feet, Harrison tucked his gun under his arm and strode away without a backward glance.

"How could I kill the little wretch when he got so chummy?" he asked himself, as if to excuse his unprofessional behaviour, and then grinned at his foolishness.

After he had gone a short distance, something impelled him to look behind. There, silently tracking him, and only a few yards away, was the dingo pup.

"Well I'll be hanged!" exclaimed the amazed bushman. He stood until the pup came up to him and then, stooping down, picked it up without any protest from Warrigal.

"All right, if this is the way you want it," he told the pup. "Don't say I didn't warn you. I'm going to take you back to my camp and murder you there."

But as he spoke, Harrison knew that that would be the last thing he would do.

CHAPTER III.

WARRIGAL'S NEW HOME.

As Harrison walked briskly along, he suddenly remembered that the cooking pot at home was empty. That had to be rectified, especially as he now had another mouth to feed.

Rectified it was, because, when almost in sight of his lonely camp, the bushman sighted a rather stout rabbit. It was feeding off a patch of grass and did not observe his approach. The fact that Warrigal was wriggling under his left arm did not hamper this keen-eyed, quick-shooting bushman. His rifle was under his right arm, but in a flash it was in the aiming position and a quick snap shot saw the fat rabbit leap convulsively into the air and then lie inert upon the patch of grass.

Collecting it on the way, Harrison proceeded to his camp, where he secured Warrigal to a small stake with a piece of rope, a proceeding to which the little dingo objected with shrill yelps.

Having skinned and cleaned the rabbit, the dog-killer popped the carcase into an old kerosene tin, which he placed on the newly-built fire. He would dine to-night from delicious rabbit stew. So would Warrigal if he fancied such food.

That Warrigal did, was proved when the meal was ready, his busy little tongue swiftly lapping up the stew that Harrison set out for him in an old empty tin.

It was while they were having their meal that they received company—two weary prospectors who dropped their heavy swags on the ground and squatted on them.

"Cheerio, mates, glad to see you," said Harrison in hearty greeting. "Get out your quart pots and have a go at the tea. Hope it's strong enough for you. Have a bit of rabbit stew, too."

"We don't want to cadge from you, mate," said one of the visitors, "but that tea would be welcome."

"Have a go at it then," the dogger invited.

The two prospectors unrolled their swags and each produced a battered quart pot. Harrison put an extra billy of water on the fire to boil, and threw a generous portion of tea into it. Tied to his stake, little Warrigal watched the coming of these new humans with interest and some awe, and his interest took vocal form with a few shrill yaps.

"What was that?" inquired one of the prospectors, Jack Lawson, pausing with a mug of tea half-way to his lips. "It sounded like a dingo pup."

"That's just what it is," returned Harrison with a smile. "I've got him tethered over there near the tent."

"What on earth for?" asked Lawson.

"Frankly, I'm blessed if I know," confessed Harrison, scratching his head. He told his visitors how he had become possessed of the little wild dog.

"I couldn't knock the little wretch on the head," he added. "I suppose I should have, but, well, I couldn't."

The other prospector, George McPherson, looked at him quizzically.

"You're the first soft-hearted dingo killer I've met," he

said, adding a quick smile that robbed the statement of any offence; "Don't you know you are letting money get away from you?"

Charlie Harrison grunted.

"I'm afraid I can't turn him into a scalp now. I guess I'd better take him back to where his mother can find him."

"Yes, the poor old lady will be worried sick," said Lawson with a roar of laughter, in which the other two men joined.

"As a matter of fact," Harrison confessed, "I'm thinking of keeping the pup and rearing him up. He should make a good dog and be handy to me in my work."

"Don't you do it, mate," said McPherson earnestly. "You'll have nothing but trouble if you start that. I've known other fellows to try to rear dingoes as pets and every one of them regretted it. So will you. Apart from anything else, you'll never hold him. He might stay with you for years, but in the end he will go back to the wilds."

"Yes," put in Lawson, "and don't forget that you won't be too popular with station owners and squatters if you trail around with a dingo, no matter how well you train him. If you train him to become familiar with humans and their ways, he will be an awful nuisance in settled areas. No, mate, knock him on the head and have done with it. You don't realise the trouble you are cooking up for yourself."

"I don't agree with that at all," said Harrison. "He is only a pup now. If I can keep him away from the dingo pack from now on, he will become domesticated—just the same as if he were a sheep dog or a cattle dog. Why should he want to return to the dingo pack?"

"Because the wild and primitive life is born in him," said McPherson. "Sheep and cattle dogs have been bred under domestic conditions for thousands of years. They are part and parcel of human life, yet sometimes they go wild. So what chance have you got with a dingo?"

"Don't the aboriginals catch dingo pups and train them to hunt when they grow up?" demanded the dogger.

"Yes, and you know the type of flea-bitten curs the aboriginals' dogs are," said Lawson scornfully.

"I'm inclined to try the experiment all the same," Harrison replied obstinately. "I figure out that if I keep him away from the pack and train him right from his puppy days, he'll be as good a dog as any domesticated animal."

"Go ahead then, but the wild will get him sooner or later. One of these fine days he will desert you and return to the pack. Think what a menace he could become. Wise in the ways of men, he could collect a dingo band and wreak havoc among sheep and cattle."

"Dingoes don't hunt in packs," retorted Harrison, more for the want of a more suitable answer.

"Quite so," agreed Lawson. "They generally live in packs, but hunt alone, or with their own particular mates. I understand, though I've never seen it myself, that occasionally they do hunt in a gang when the game is too big for one or two to handle."

"That is right," said the dogger. "They destroy sheep, calves and poultry in settled areas. In the wild country they go for the smaller animals and any birds they can catch on the ground."

"By the way," he added, "don't get the idea that I've got any love for dingoes. Isn't my job to kill them off?"

McPherson laughed. "You don't seem to have enough courage to kill off that little yelper you have tied to the stake over there," he grinned.

"Dingoes," said his friend Lawson, "are a dashed nuisance and should all be killed. They are a cowardly lot of animals."

"Not always," said Harrison. "They won't attack man—at

least I've never heard of any cases, but of course there is no knowing what a fierce dingo might do if he were cornered and had to fight for his life. They say that even a worm will turn if the provocation is strong enough."

"I don't suppose there are very many purebred dingoes these days," McPherson said as he lit his pipe with a stick from the fire. "Many domestic dogs have gone wild and I suppose most of the dingoes now are half-breeds."

"There are plenty of both and I've met them," said the dogger. "I haven't much respect for the true dingo because he isn't as wise as some people try to make out. It is a different matter, though, when he mates with domestic animals, especially Alsatians. It is then that they become very cunning and very dangerous too."

"By the way," he added, "I don't think the pup there is a pure breed."

"And yet, in spite of that, you are going to take it and raise it among domestic dogs. Mate, you don't know what you are doing. Knock the little devil on the head and have done with it," advised Lawson.

"No," said Harrison gruffly.

"Would you like me to do it for you?" asked the prospector.

"Certainly not," was the terse answer.

"How is business with you? Getting plenty of scalps?" asked McPherson, anxious to change the subject. He sensed growing resentment on the part of the dogger and he did not want any unpleasantness. As far as he was concerned personally, he did not care what fate held in store for the dingo pup.

"I can't complain," said Harrison. "I have a good few, and to-morrow I'm going into town to turn them into money. Then I think I'll have a holiday somewhere."

"With the pup?"

"Yes. With the pup."

"I've picked up a few pounds myself with an odd scalp or two," remarked McPherson. "I've always had to do it the hard way though. I've never had Chinaman's luck."

Harrison grinned. "So you know the story of the Chinese dogger, eh?" he laughed. "Yes, he must have been a cunning chap," said McPherson with an answering laugh.

Lawson, looking interested, demanded to be let into the joke.

"It happened many years ago out west," said the dingo-killer. "At that time, the Government was paying £1 each for scalps. There weren't many dingoes in that particular area until the Chinaman arrived."

"How did he increase them? Did he bring a pack with him?"

"Not quite," laughed Harrison. "He asked the station owner for a job as a dogger, and was engaged. He vanished for a time and then came back with a scalp and collected his £1. Off he went again and soon returned with another. After that he began to bring them in by the dozen and the station people started to scratch their heads. They had seen a few dingoes about, but no big packs like the Chinese must have met. They thought he had run into a big pack and used a machine gun on them.

"Anyway, the mystery was solved," went on Harrison with a hearty chuckle. "Somebody at the station got suspicious and examined the scalps very carefully. Know what he discovered? That Chinaman had been making his own scalps and doing an excellent job of it. When he killed a dingo he used his Oriental arts on it and succeeded in manufacturing dozens of scalps, ears and all."

"What happened to him?" asked Lawson.

"I never heard, but it forced the authorities to alter the

scheme of things. In those days a scalp alone did them, but now a scalp means a strip of skin cut from the tip of the dog's nose right down to the back of the tail."

"But how does that get over it?" inquired the prospector.

"Well, mate, even a magician couldn't make half a dozen backbones out of one dingo," laughed Harrison.

"I knew a chap up in Northern Queensland who used to hunt dingoes on horseback and kill them with his stirrup iron," put in Lawson, not to be left out of the stories, "he was a marvellous horseman as most outback Australians are. He used to go out round about dusk when the dingoes were coming down out of the hills, and when he sighted one in an open space, which wasn't often of course, he used to chase it on his horse, unhook one of his stirrup irons, leather strap and all, and use it as a hand sling. He'd ride the dingo down and crack him on the head with the swinging iron."

"I'll bet he did!" scoffed Harrison.

"It is a fact," said Lawson earnestly. "I've yet to see what an outback Australian cannot do on a horse... American cowboys are children compared with them."

"I don't doubt you, but there must be dingoes and dingoes and horses and horses," said McPherson. "Which reminds me of that old poem written by Will H. Ogilvie. We used to recite it at school:

"'For K. G. or coronet, kingdom or crown,
The boys on Kalangada care not a rap;
But the honour they ask for is galloping down
The red and white dingo of Brigalow Gap.
He has beaten us fairly at every exchange;
He is hard to keep up with and harder to track.
He knows every stone on the Brigalow Range. —
The fastest and wildest and worst of the pack.'"

"Some dingo," commented Harrison. "I'd like to get him over the sights of my rifle. As for riding him down, friend Lawson here can do that with his stirrup iron."

"Just a moment," protested McPherson. "Let me finish it."

> *"Good horses behind him with rowels we've*
>   *raked:*
> *On Bogan the bushcrows are feasting their fill,*
> *And Footstep is foundered and Starlight is staked,*
> *But the red and white dingo makes light of us still.*
> *For him a fast gallop is nothing but fun.—*
> *Too cunning to poison, too wary to trap,*
> *You can't get the sight of a rifle or gun*
> *On the red and white dingo of Brigalow Gap.'"*

"Be that as it may," commented Harrison, "I'd still like to have a go at him. I've never had a dingo beat me yet."

"Not so far, perhaps," said McPherson meaningly, as he threw a glance at little Warrigal squatting near his stake.

CHAPTER IV.
THE MISSING BABY.

WARRIGAL, anchored securely to that stake near the dogger's tent, could not keep his eyes off the three men at the fire. The leaping flames intrigued him vastly. He had never seen a fire before and he wondered what it could be.

Harrison's camp was situated on the only piece of elevated ground in a gully, rocked in by steep hills on three sides and with the open plains in front. It was his habit each day to make the rounds of many traps and also to examine poison baits he had laid. Sometimes he managed to shoot a dog with his rifle, but not often as this country was wild and rugged, offering splendid natural hiding places for the cunning dingoes.

As the men sat conversing round the fire and telling each other anecdotes of the bush and the plains, their talk was interrupted by a long drawn out howl, coming from the cliffs above them. Its effect upon young Warrigal was electrical. Throwing back his head he gave several shrill yaps and endeavoured to imitate the dismal howl. His vocal chords, however, were not equal to the task, the result being a long whine, but sad enough.

"Shut up, you noisy little devil!" shouted McPherson,

but the pup took no notice of him. As the dingo on the rocks above gave tongue again, it was joined by a second wild dog, the duet making the echoes ring eerily.

"Most likely that is dad and mother looking for their lost son," suggested Lawson. "The little chap seems to recognise their voices."

Harrison climbed to his feet and stared upwards. For a time he could see nothing, and then his keen eyes detected the source of the wild dog serenade.

"There they are," he said. "Look, up there on that big boulder over to the right. I can just make them out. It is a pity the moon is in the wrong direction. They make a difficult target from here."

"Have a shot at them in any case," said McPherson. "If they really are the pup's parents, we'll get no sleep to-night. They'll howl around the camp until dawn."

"If you intend to keep that pup, you'd better see that he is securely tied up," advised Lawson. "Look at him."

Warrigal, having recognised the voices of his father and mother, was putting up a great struggle, pulling and twisting in a fruitless endeavour to rid himself of a rope that had become positively hateful. He had not minded it so much after the first irksomeness had passed, because there had been so many strange and unusual things to engross him; but realisation had now returned to him in a flood. He was just a little pup, the captive of a human being, and he wanted his mother.

That his mother wanted him too, was clear. She was calling to him, and so was his father, though the old man Dingo was not so persistently vocal.

Unable to stand the howling any longer, Harrison entered his tent and came outside with his rifle. It was a difficult shot. The two old dingoes could be discerned faintly on the edge of the cliff, perhaps 200 feet up. They were partly in shadow, and it was only when they moved slightly that the men below could see them at all.

Sighting the rifle as best he could, the dogger pulled the trigger. There was a loud report and the howling dingoes became mute in mid-yap.

"Missed them both," said Harrison ruefully. "It doesn't matter, though. I'll be satisfied if the shot scares them away. I know plenty of sweeter lullabies to put me to sleep than a couple of howling dingoes."

"You'll have to do something about the pup," said Lawson. "He's likely to yelp all night now."

Harrison looked down uncertainly at the struggling Warrigal, half-inclined to untie him and let him go. The pup was trying to commit suicide by twisting himself into a knot in an effort to get rid of the rope. The dogger bent down and patted him, to be rewarded with a sharp nip on the hand.

"The little villain bit me!" exclaimed Harrison. "I've a good mind to brain him."

"That's what we've been telling you to do all along," said McPherson. "No good will come of keeping him."

It needed just that remark to stiffen the dogger's resolve. "No, I'm keeping him," he replied tersely.

With a wary eye on the struggling pup, he bent down, grabbed it by the scruff of the neck with one hand, and placed the other over its small muzzle, stifling its yelps. As he held the pup, Lawson untied the rope. Carrying Warrigal by the scruff of the neck, Harrison took him inside the tent and dumped him in an old wooden box. Across this he placed a piece of board, leaving a generous gap for air, and then he put a large stone on top of the board.

"No chance of his escaping from that prison," said the dogger with satisfaction, as indignant but muffled yelps penetrated from the box. Warrigal snuffled and yelped for a minute or so before accepting the inevitable and becoming silent.

Shortly afterwards, the three men retired for the night, Harrison to the bunk in his tent and the two prospectors to the side of the dying fire where, rolled in their blankets, they were soon asleep.

Lying in his bunk, Harrison gave himself up to thought. He was undecided just what to do about young Warrigal. If he followed his original plan, he would break camp on the following day and leave for the township to realise on his large pile of dingo scalps and rabbit skins. Later he intended to stay a few days with his married sister, who lived in a town down south. She might not fancy having a dingo pup at the house, but there would be no need for him to tell her the little chap's history. She knew nothing about dogs. Perhaps he could leave Warrigal with her for a few months so that he would grow accustomed to town dogs and so forget his wild parents and his earlier upbringing.

But would that ruin him as a hunting dog? Harrison told himself that he did not want any tame town dogs with him when he was hunting. It was a worrying problem.

As the dingo-hunter turned the matter over and over in his mind, he became drowsy, and finally fell asleep, the problem unsolved. Like most bushmen he was not a heavy sleeper. What woke him he did not know, but at once he became aware of whining noises issuing from the box at the side of the bunk. He smiled to himself. Only little Warrigal feeling a bit restless. He closed his eyes and then opened them again. His keen ears had detected sounds outside the tent.

Sitting up quietly, he looked at the pale moonlit patch of earth, rocks and scrub visible beyond the raised flap of the tent. At first he saw nothing, and then he became aware of movement among bushes directly opposite. Something was there—perhaps a rabbit.

With his gaze riveted on the spot, he was rewarded with a quick glimpse of a shadowy figure crouched under the bush. As he watched, he saw the figure move and noticed two shining lights pointing in his direction. He knew what they were-the eyes of some nocturnal animal; and if his bushman's instincts did not betray him, they belonged to a dingo, and a big dingo, too! It would be Warrigal's father or mother, perhaps both.

Quietly he leaned from the bunk and took hold of his big rifle which was always near at hand and loaded. With the weapon held ready, he kept his eyes glued on the shadowy form. Again came the slight rustle that had first attracted his attention to the bush, and he saw a big dingo step quietly from cover and stand revealed in the pale rays of the setting moon.

The wild dog advanced a few feet and then stopped dead, its head slowly turning from side to side as it surveyed it's surroundings. Harrison sat fascinated, making no attempt to aim the gun. He felt that if he fired at it he could hardly miss at that range, even though the light was not ideal for shooting; but he was content to await events. How close would the wild dog actually come?

The dingo, however, was in no hurry. It stood immobile in the one spot for minutes on end before it took a few more stealthy paces forward.

Warrigal's mother, for it was she, was prey to conflicting emotions. There was collie as well as dingo in her, but her whole training from puppyhood had taught her the need for the utmost caution in every act. From her collie father she had inherited gentleness not often apparent in the full-blooded dingo, but, above all else, she had that fierce mother-love and urge to protect her young possessed by all dogs, wild or domesticated.

She and her mate had returned from the pack hunt to find Warrigal missing. She had searched frantically for him all around the home cave, without success. Then chance took her down into the gully into which Warrigal had fallen, and there she had come across his scent. Following it down the ravine and out on to the plains, she was aghast to discover it mixed with the terrible man-scent, the worst known to her. In her trailing she lost Warrigal's scent altogether. That was where Harrison had picked up the youngster to carry. She quested far and wide in a frantic effort to recover the scent, but without avail, so had returned disconsolately to the home cave where her mate was awaiting her, quite convinced that her pup had become the victim of a marauding human monster.

Though he sympathised with her, the old dingo had not felt called upon to search for the errant puppy. His own father and mother had thrown him out into the world at an early age to fend for himself, and in his opinion it was high time that young Warrigal got out and earned his own living. That the pup was a little young yet to do that, did not worry the old man dingo. In these parts it was every dog for itself. It was no place for molly-coddles. When night fell the two dingoes left their cave together for the nightly hunt, and in their questings, reached the rise overlooking Harrison's camp. Sometimes it was possible to secure an easy meal among the bushes here. An absence of high trees forced birds to roost in the low bushes, and many a time the dingoes had succeeded in catching some roosting bird, pulling it from a branch and eating it without the bird waking up.

As they poked around among the bushes, the mother dingo

stopped short and cocked a listening ear. From somewhere down below had come to her a familiar sound—the voice of her missing pup. The old man dingo caught the sound too, and they both sneaked silently through the bushes until they reached a rock overlooking the dingo hunter's camp.

Though filled with anxiety for the safety of her pup, the mother dingo was not so foolish as to dash to his assistance. She merely set up a howl to let him know that she was near. Her mate joined in the chorus, but both became mute as a loud report sounded from the camp and a bullet whistled between them.

It was more than enough for the old man dingo. He had had his experiences of men and their guns, and had no desire to seek closer acquaintance with either. The report of the shot was still echoing on the silent night as he faded among the rocks and bushes, heading with all speed back to his home cave and safety.

Though the mother dingo also left the spot like a tawny ghost, she did not go far. Warrigal was her only pup, and she was not yet ready to surrender him to the wilds. She took a long circuitous route down out of the high places to the flat country, and returned in the direction of the camp, making every use of available cover.

She came into view of the camp and was slightly reassured by the dead silence. The fire had died down to the faintest red gleam. She noted two heaps beside it, and knew them instantly for humans. Withdrawing into the bushes, she slunk round until the tent hid them from her view. That did not actually dispose of them as menaces to her safety, but they were out of her sight and she drew some comfort from that.

When she emerged from the bushes again, she was directly opposite the tent opening. Her keen eyes searched everywhere, but she could see no sign of Warrigal. When viewing the camp from the rocks above before the bullet had sent her flying, she had seen the pup tied to a stake outside the tent. He was not there now. Then where was he?

Crouching back under the friendly bush, she gave the matter intense thought. She was brave enough in ordinary circumstances, but shrank from the prospect of having to search every inch of the white man's territory for her son.

Warrigal himself saved her that terrifying task. In the stifling darkness of his box, he began to sniffle and whine. Instantly his mother tensed. Low as the sounds were, her keen ears picked them up. So the pup was in the tent itself. This was going to be a super-dingo task, she told herself. She knew the tent was occupied by a human. Her keen scent told her that.

Impelled by her mother-love and her yearning for her pup, the wild dog cautiously left the sheltering bush and advanced a few paces towards the tent, every sense keyed up and on the alert—ready to fly for her life should the least thing untoward occur.

Harrison in his bunk watched her, fascinated, wondering if she intended to enter the tent.

And then his professional instincts overcame him. There, only a few yards away, was a dingo scalp for the taking. It would be very easy money.

Slowly he raised his rifle and took steady aim. The dingo was now standing stock still, sharp muzzle pointed straight in his direction and eyes shining luminously.

Suddenly he saw her head swing sharply to the right and in a moment she had vanished—vanished as if she had been smoke dissipated by a sharp puff of wind. Harrison lowered his gun in astonishment.

"What on earth happened to her?" he said aloud.

"She spotted me and bolted," came a voice from outside the tent, and Lawson poked his head around the flap. "I woke up and saw a big dingo creeping into the tent and as I jumped up she went for her life. I never saw anything move so fast."

Lawson entered the tent and sat down on the bunk. Dawn was not far off and neither of the men could see any sense in going back to bed again. They began to smoke and yarn.

As for Warrigal's mother, she was swiftly working her way up through the rocks and scrub to the home cave, her heart heavy with the firm conviction that her pup was lost to her forever. She would never have the courage again to visit that camp in search of him.

CHAPTER V.
THE RABBIT COUNTRY.

DAWN found the camp a hive of industry. While McPherson built up the fire and prepared breakfast, Lawson assisted Harrison to dismantle his tent and pack his gear into the old spring cart. Harrison had a horse, which he both rode and drove, stabled several hundreds of yards from the camp in a huge cave hollowed out of the sandstone by the winds and storms of centuries.

Everything was in readiness for the journey to the township before the men sat down to their morning meal.

"I've decided not to go to the town where my sister lives, at least not straight away," Harrison told the prospectors. "I'll drop my load of scalps and skins at the township and arrange for my cheque. Then I think I'll head south and spend a few months trapping rabbits, I know a good stretch of country, free from dingoes, where young Warrigal will have a chance to forget his parents."

"He'll never do that," said McPherson. "Once a dingo, always a dingo."

"That is something I intend to disprove," said Harrison gruffly.

The two prospectors accepted with gratitude the dogger's

invitation to ride with him to the small township, which was about 30 miles away. The trip would be slow, but their time was their own. Harrison had released Warrigal from the box before dismantling the tent and he was not tied to the stake again. The pup took a keen interest in everything that was going on, and seemed to have forgotten, for the time being anyway, the happenings of the night.

As they drove away from the old camp, Warrigal, standing on a heap of skins in the spring cart, quivered with excitement at his first ride.

Harrison and his friends pursued their way leisurely, camping and shooting as the fancy took them, and it was two days before they reached the small township. This consisted of a police station, a small store and a few shacks, the latter occupied by the families of drovers and of stockmen who worked on neighboring sheep stations.

When Harrison visited the police station to arrange for the disposal of his scalps, he left Warrigal in the box with the board on top of it. He intended to take fine care the police trooper did not see the pup. Dingoes, especially half-bred ones, were noxious animals to be shot on sight. Their use as pets was not encouraged.

His business concluded with the trooper, who did not even leave his office, Harrison joined McPherson and Lawson at the store. Here he laid in a fresh stock of provisions. The two prospectors would await the arrival of the weekly mail car and return in it to civilisation for a short holiday before setting out again on another prospecting trip.

Bidding his two friends a cheery farewell, the dogger left the township. His destination now was a large sheep station many miles southwards. Here he knew that the proprietor would welcome him with open arms. Rabbits were always numerous on the property, and although the station hands did their best to keep them in check with trap, gun and poison, an extra man, with nothing to do but kill rabbits was always assured of a welcome.

The dogger pitched his camp on the banks of a pretty little creek which meandered through the property to join the river eight or nine miles farther down. After he had fixed everything to his satisfaction, including the hobbling of his horse and the secure tethering of Warrigal to one leg of the bunk in the tent, he took his gun and went off down the creek to shoot his dinner. He was lucky to secure a wild duck in a small lagoon, or excavated waterhole, and returned to camp in triumph.

Some hours later, he saddled his horse and rode the five miles to the station homestead—where, as he anticipated, he received a warm welcome from the owner, old Mr. Jacobs, who gave him his heartiest permission to kill all the rabbits he could get hold of.

Harrison made up his mind to stay on the property for several months. During that period he seldom appeared at the homestead, and on those rare occasions, Warrigal was left in the closed tent. As a precaution against the dog's discovery, the bushman never camped in the one spot longer that a week at a time, and always at least half a dozen miles from the homestead.

Out on the huge runs, or in the hills, Warrigal was his constant companion, and Harrison was at great pains to train him.

As time went on, the dog learned how to run down and catch rabbits for his master, killing silently, but never eating the little animals. He also tackled other game such as small kangaroos, bandicoots and ground birds, learning from the bushman what his own parents, or his own natural instinct would have taught him in any case.

The pup was growing apace and promised to be a very handsome dog. He had the sharp muzzle and stiff ears of his dingo ancestors, but the white chest and white feet of his collie grandfather. His coat was nearer red than brown or yellow, and the last six inches of his bushy tail were white.

As the dog grew, Harrison became certain that he was not a full-blooded dingo, though he had always suspected it. The dogger felt confident, too, that he would not be recognised as a wild dog descendant in any place other than the out back; not even there, perhaps.

Though he had inherited several of his collie ancestor's characteristics, there was one important trait that he had not—a part that allied him for all time with the dingoes— he was unable to bark. As far as that went, Warrigal was a singularly silent dog. If he did not bark, neither did he howl so mournfully or yelp so much as the true dingo. Perhaps, Harrison thought, that was because there were no other wild dogs in the country where they now were.

And as the days passed into weeks and weeks into months, Harrison and Warrigal became very much attached to each other. The bushman found it easy to train him to become a first rate rabbit hunter, and though at first Warrigal had been averse to hunting during the day preferring the dusk and the night as the dingoes did—the dogger gradually got him into the habit; or thought he did. Certainly, Warrigal did what was expected of him when the sun was in the sky— working for his master as an efficient rabbit killer—but at night, when the stars were in the heavens and Harrison was fast asleep in his bunk, the dog went out on business of his own, stalking and killing with the swiftness and silence of death itself.

Harrison knew nothing of this until, emerging from his tent one morning, he found two dead rabbits lying outside.

It did not require a minute examination of the carcases to prove to him that Warrigal had killed them.

Though he patted the dog for its extra work, the bushman was concerned. He did not want to have to tie Warrigal up at nights, but if the dog was wandering the countryside during the hours of darkness, trouble might come of it. What if Warrigal paid visits to the station homestead and created havoc in the fowlyard, or killed lambs? After all, he was part-dingo, and likely to break out, though the bushman hated to admit that even to himself.

"I suppose I'll have to tie you up," he said gloomily. "Can't run any risks you know. I'd hate to lose you now, old boy."

Warrigal pricked up his ears at the sound of the man's voice, and lazily thumped his tail on the ground.

That night the bushman did tie him up before he went to bed. In the morning there were three dead rabbits outside the tent and Warrigal was lying contentedly in the shade of a big gum tree. Around his neck was a short bit of rope with the end chewed. The rest of the rope was still tied to the stake driven in the ground near the tree trunk.

"So you used your teeth on it, did you?" muttered the dogger. "All right, my lad, next time I'm in town I'll buy you a good strong chain."

He did not trouble to tie the dog up after this episode, and though once or twice there were dead rabbits outside the camp of a morning, no complaints came to him of marauding dingoes. The station property covered thousands of acres and as they did not stop in the one spot for long, Harrison guessed that Warrigal had never troubled to visit the homestead. There was always new country to interest him.

One morning while they were working along the creek bank, they met a black kelpie dog. Harrison recognised it as the property of Mr. Jacobs. Anxiously he looked in all directions, fearing that the kelpie had a human companion who might take an inconvenient interest in Warrigal. Nobody was in sight, however, so Harrison concluded, with relief, that the dog was out on a stroll by itself.

But though there was no other human being to take an interest in the dingo, the kelpie did. It advanced belligerently, making throaty growls. Warrigal eyed it with interest, but did not advance to meet it; he was however very much on the alert.

"Buzz off, you, go on home," Harrison yelled at the kelpie which, disregarding him, stalked, stiff-legged and with back hair bristling, right up to Warrigal and began to sniff him. Warrigal sniffed back, and the kelpie snarled menacingly.

"Hang it all, don't you two start to fight," pleaded the anxious dogger, searching around frantically for a stick. He found one, but before he could use it, the kelpie attacked Warrigal, biting him savagely on the neck. Surprised and hurt, the red and white dog drew back a pace, but the kelpie, its blood fully up, bit him on the flank.

With a throaty snarl, a sound that Harrison had never heard him give before, Warrigal grappled with the kelpie, all his latent, primitive savagery uppermost. With the stick still grasped in his hand, but too astounded to use it, Harrison watched the struggle. The two dogs were now rolling over and over, biting and scratching, savage teeth lacerating and tearing flesh and hide. The kelpie was snarling, yelping and growling, but Warrigal was almost completely silent.

It struck the bushman that there was something very sinister in his pet's behaviour. Unquestionably, he was a deadly killer. The kelpie was a game fighter, but he did not possess the awful strength of jaw that his antagonist had. The dingo's bite could rend and tear flesh while the kelpie's equivalent effort could do no more than inflict a superficial wound. The kelpie would have withdrawn from the fight more than once, but Warrigal would not allow him.

When he tackled the dingo, the black station dog made the last and greatest mistake of his life. He was a domesticated animal, accustomed to fighting his fellow kelpies and sheep dogs. These fights might be vicious contests when actually waged, but they were not deadly. There was no menace in them. They were battles to while away the time or to repay some real or fancied slight.

With Warrigal it was different. He was a dog born and bred in the wilds, where survival was the prize for the fittest. The dingo pack did not fight battles for the fun of the thing. Life was a serious business and when combat was joined, it was a fight to the death.

It will never be known what had actuated the kelpie in tackling Warrigal. Perhaps he had intended only to show a stranger that it couldn't walk with impunity over land which belonged to the kelpie and his master; perhaps he had had an instinctive distrust of this stranger; perhaps he had been in need of a little exercise. But whatever the reason, it can be assumed that the station dog had had no intention of fighting a battle of supremacy, with death the sad prize of the loser.

When Warrigal got his teeth into the kelpie's throat, the battle was at an end. Far too late Harrison came to life and began furiously to beat Warrigal with the stick. The dingo was on top with his fangs buried in the kelpie's throat, but the stick made no impression upon him. He was completely submerged in his blood lust.

Throwing the stick aside, Harrison seized Warrigal by the scruff of the neck with both hands, and literally dragged him from his stricken adversary...

Harrison, with Warrigal looking on, buried the kelpie

in a deep rabbit warren in the side of the creek bank. It was a sorrowful task. The man mourned over the death of the black dog, and he mourned over the possible effects on Warrigal. Of course, the dingo had killed numerous rabbits, a few small kangaroos and wallabies, but that was merely hunting business. Now that he had killed another dog, what next might he tackle? Throughout the long months they had been wandering together, he had, with no little ingenuity, succeeded in keeping Warrigal hidden away from other dogs and other humans. He wanted the dingo to forget the wilds and his early upbringing. Now it would seem that all his good work had gone for nothing.

"Warrigal, my lad," he said as they made their way back to their camp, "you've done it now. There is nothing for us to do but move on."

Warrigal, who was feeling mighty proud of himself, gave no indication of having heard his master. As he walked at the bushman's heels, the dingo was a prey to conflicting emotions. Deep down inside him was stirring the blood of a thousand warring ancestors, each one of them a hunter and a killer. The fight with the kelpie had been forced upon him. It was his first fight, but instinct had told him how to wage the battle. He had won. It was a great feeling, and Warrigal trod on air as he trotted at the heels of the worried Harrison.

And the bushman was worried. He had made up his mind not to say anything to Mr. Jacobs about the dead kelpie. He realised that it was his duty to tell the station owner. Jacobs had been friendly and hospitable towards him, and it would be just common decency and courtesy to tell him about the kelpie's death. But if he did that, Harrison pondered, it would most likely be the end of Warrigal. He could not bear to lose his pet, so he decided to say nothing. Instead, he would ride over to the homestead and tell Jacobs that he was taking his skins to town. He would tell him that he would return and continue his rabbiting.

Harrison had no intention of returning. But where would he go? Back to the dingo country? Certainly not! Once Warrigal was among those dingo-infested hills, now that he had tasted blood in combat the first howls of the hunting pack would find him back with them.

"I'll go to see my sister and I'll take Warrigal with me," he said aloud.

Warrigal pricked up his ears, but made no comment.

His mind made up, Harrison did not delay visiting the station owner. Leaving Warrigal securely tied to the leg of the bunk in the closed tent, a situation in which experience had taught him the dog would remain silent for hours, the dogger saddled his horse and rode off. Old Mr. Jacobs was sitting on the side verandah reading a magazine and waved a friendly hand as Harrison rode up and dismounted.

"How is the job going, Charlie?" he inquired as the dogger mounted the verandah. "I hope you haven't left too many rabbits in the back paddocks?"

"I'm afraid there are a few there, Mr. Jacobs," smiled the bushman. "I can't complain, though. I've got a whole stack of skins and I've just dropped over to tell you that I'll be taking this lot to town to-morrow. It has been good of you, shifting them for me in the past, Mr. Jacobs, but I'll take this lot in myself."

"You'll be coming back, I hope?"

"Oh, yes, sure," said Harrison quickly. "I've not made my fortune yet. With the price of skins as high as it is, I intend to pile up all I can."

"Good for you son!" complimented the station owner. "By the way, Charlie," he said, after a slight pause, "in your wanderings over the paddocks and runs, have you seen any dingoes about?"

"Hey? Dingoes?" ejaculated the startled bushman.

"Yes, dingoes! You know what dingoes are, don't you?" chuckled the old man. "I seem to have heard somewhere that you are an expert dingo-killer."

"Oh, yes, I think I could tell a dingo if I saw one," said Harrison with a feeble smile. "No, I haven't seen any around here. Why do you ask?"

"Because I heard one howling the other night."

"You what?" exclaimed Harrison. "Are you sure? It might have been one of your sheep dogs."

"Look here, young fellow, don't you try to make out that an old-timer like I am don't know a dingo's howl when he hears it," snorted the station boss. "I tell you I heard a dingo howling the other night. I was in bed, and if you tell me that I dreamed it, I'll throw this magazine at you."

"I've never seen or heard any dingoes in this country, and I've been over practically every inch of it," said the bushman, inwardly cursing Warrigal and his nocturnal prowlings. "Was the howl near at hand?"

"It was both near and far," replied Jacobs. "I heard it several times. Now look here, Charlie, I don't want any dingoes hanging around here and I am willing to pay a high price for this one's scalp. Get him before he has a chance to do any damage, and I'll make it well worth your while."

"All right, Mr. Jacobs. I'll set traps and baits and keep a sharp eye out for it as soon as I return from town," said the dogger, at the same time mentally registering the fact that there would be no prowling dingoes around the station after he and Warrigal had departed.

"I can't make it out at all," went on the station owner. "we have never had any dingoes closer than the ranges, and they must be a hundred miles away. Maybe it is some old man killer that has deserted the pack and has set up in business on his own. I don't like it, Charlie. I've had too much experience with these lone killers."

"Yes, they can be nuisances," said the dogger, wishing that Jacobs would change the subject, or let him get away. The old station boss, however, was wound up, and intended to complete his lecture.

"Listen here, my boy," he said, "I've known a single old man dingo to kill over thirty sheep in one night. Why did he have to do that? It wasn't hunger, because all he did was to tear the wool off three of them and eat out their kidneys."

"Perhaps he wanted to keep the others for future feeds," ventured Harrison.

"Are you trying to be funny?" roared old Jacobs. "Who ever heard of a dingo having a refrigerator? I tell you it was just plain viciousness and downright nastiness. And I won't have it happen here, see?"

"No, certainly not, Mr. Jacobs," said the dogger soothingly. "I'll do what I can to get rid of him for you."

"Good, and any foxes you see about, too."

"I haven't sighted any," said Harrison.

"Then you must be going blind," snorted Jacobs. "There are very few, thank goodness, but I've seen 'em around. We used to have a lot, but we got rid of 'em."

"Have you lost any sheep through foxes?"

"You bet I have," grunted Jacobs. "They go fer the lambs. I've seen them stalking sheep in the lambing season. They hunt the ewes away, doing the job very quietly, and then collect any lambs that have become lost."

"Foxes are not easy to get," said Harrison, making conversation. He wanted to get back to his camp and had no interest in foxes.

"You'll find them in the rabbit warrens, Charlie. I've dug out burrows and found the bones of dead lambs and fowls. And don't try to tell me that the rabbits carted them there. Cunning little beggars, foxes. You try hunting one with a gun. He's a sneaky little devil, trotting along as if he is scared of nothing and as if his tail is too heavy to carry. Yes, and he has the impudence to stop every now and then and look back at you like a cat."

"I've seen them," said Harrison briefly, casting around desperately for an excuse to get away from the garrulous old chap.

"Know how they get into the rabbit burrows?" demanded Jacobs. "They hear the young rabbits crying like kittens and just dig down into the earth, following the sound. Then they eat the young rabbits and breed there themselves. I've seen fox cubs in rabbit burrows many a time."

"So have I. Well, Mr. Jacobs, I must be leaving. Thanks for everything. I'll see you when I get back from town," said the bushman wearily.

"All right then, Charlie," said the old man, walking to the edge of the verandah and watching the agile bushman mount his horse.

"Don't forget that dingo when you get back!" he shouted after the retreating horseman.

"I won't. So long!" Harrison shouted back and, urging his horse to a gallop, he made straight for his camp by the creek.

CHAPTER VI.
A WILD DOG GOES TO TOWN.

WHEN Charlie Harrison left the station property in his old spring cart laden with his worldly goods, which included Warrigal lying lazily upon a heap of rabbit skins, he did not head for the township where he had parted from the two prospectors nearly eighteen months earlier. He was not going to risk jeopardising his dog's future. Warrigal was nearly full-grown now, and thus harder to conceal than he had been as a pup. Certainly, he could not be dumped unceremoniously in a box.

The bushman intended to make his way southwards towards the town where his sister lived. That town was many miles away and there, he felt, Warrigal would be safe. While staying with his sister for a few weeks, he would allow Warrigal to absorb town life, and then he would return to the dingo country to resume his dogging.

Proceeding leisurely, and keeping away from settlements and station properties, the bushman eventually reached the outskirts of the town in which his sister lived. As he had camped on the trip and had not visited any villages or homesteads, he had been unable to write to or wire his sister of his pending visit. He smiled to himself as he visualised her surprise when he drove up in the old cart. He had not seen his sister or her husband for over three years.

When about two miles from the town, Harrison stopped the cart and jumped down. Warrigal, without invitation, jumped down too.

"This is where I start to educate you to town life, old boy," the dogger told his pet.

Taking a length of stout rope from the cart, Harrison crawled underneath the vehicle and tied one end to the centre of the axle. Emerging again, he tied the other end to Warrigal's neck. The dog did not understand, and made a few determined efforts to pull free; but the rope was too strong.

Leaving him on the ground, Harrison climbed back on to the cart and set the horse in motion. As he drove slowly for a few yards, he glanced back and saw what he expected—Warrigal at the end of the rope sitting well back on his haunches as if he would pull the cart to a stop. As the horse kept on going, the dingo began to slide forward on his tail through the dust. He put up with this indignity for a few seconds and then got up off his tail, to be pulled willy nilly, along the track.

Harrison stopped the cart, and Warrigal immediately trotted under it. Again the bushman started off, and the exact same programme was repeated—Warrigal being dragged along sitting on his tail for a few yards and then at an unwilling walk.

"Get under the cart, you fool, and trot along with it like a sensible bush dog!" roared Harrison, as he pulled up. Warrigal at once trotted under the cart and the dogger set the horse in motion, this time driving as slowly as possible. When he looked behind, there was no sign of the dog.

"So you have caught the idea at last, have you?" shouted the bushman. "Good for you, old timer."

He gradually increased the pace of the horse until it developed into a smart walk. There was no sign now of Warrigal being towed along behind so, with a sigh of relief, Harrison kept on going.

Warrigal, trotting along underneath the cart, had, indeed, caught the idea; and he viewed the scenery as well as he could between the moving legs of the horse in front and between the revolving spokes of the wheels on either side.

Deeming it wise to reach his sister's home by a back way in preference to a crowded main street where the bush-bred dog might be terrified by passing traffic, Harrison selected the most deserted streets, meeting nothing that might perturb Warrigal. Several carts passed, but no cars. It was rather late in the day, and traffic in these back streets was at a minimum; also, there were no dogs about, for which Harrison was thankful.

At length he reached a short lane and turned the cart into it. Arriving at a double gate, he jumped down stiffly from his seat, opened the gates and led the horse through into the yard. Closing the gates and throwing a warning word to Warrigal to be still, he marched up to the back door of the house and knocked heavily.

The door was opened by a pleasant-faced woman who gave a cry of delight when she saw the bushman.

"Well, if it isn't Charlie, home from the bush!"

Quickly she grabbed him round the shoulders and planted a loud kiss on his cheek, Harrison returning the embrace affectionately.

Freeing herself from her brother's grasp, Mrs. Reece called out loudly over her shoulder: "Harry, come out and see who is here!"

There was the sound of a chair being pushed back and presently a tall man came to the door. When he saw Harrison he gave a shout of welcome and held out his hand.

"Charlie Harrison, you old son-of-a-gun! Where on earth did you spring from? Why didn't you let us know you were coming? How long are you staying this time? Where have you been all these years? Are you on your own?"

"Here, I say, Harry, one question at a time," laughed the bushman. "I'm fresh from the rabbit country and I'm all alone except for my horse and my dog."

"Well, don't stand out there. Come on in and have a feed," exclaimed Reece. "It's years since we saw you."

"Wait a moment," said the bushman. "What about the horse and cart? I can't leave them standing in the yard! Also, what about my old dog?"

"Come on in and have a cup of tea, anyway," said his sister. "Then Harry can help you unload your things. You can put the horse in the paddock across the lane and the cart can go into the shed. As for the dog, well he can have the old kennel in the corner. It's empty, except for a few spiders. I hope he isn't a particular kind of dog? Not stuck up, or fastidious?"

"Not him," laughed Harrison. "He's a treasure! What is more he doesn't bark at all."

"Quite a miracle dog, eh?"

"Not really. It is just the way I have trained him. Barking dogs are no good when you are out hunting," said Harrison.

As they sat down to tea, Mrs. Reece and her husband plied him with questions. Harry Reece was a town man, a hairdresser by occupation, and knew nothing about the bush, the plains or the ranges. His wife also had scant knowledge of those places. Charlie Harrison had been a wanderer since boyhood, and his sister, being much attached to him, was anxious to know how he had been faring in the three years since they last had met.

"You look in the best of health, Charlie," she said, and Harrison replied that he felt good, too.

"Do you plan to stay long?" Harry Reece asked.

"Well, Harry I've got a fair stack of skins to dispose of while I am here. Then I think I'll take a trip to the city for a few days. If I do, will you mind looking after my horse and dog while I'm down there? Neither will be the least trouble to you. "

"Only too delighted, Charlie," said Reece warmly. "By the way, what is the dog's name?"

"Er, oh, I call him Warrigal," said Harrison, a little uneasily.

"That's a nice name, but a strange one," commented Reece. "Is it an aboriginal word?"

"Yes, and it means 'dingo'," said the bushman deliberately.

"Go on, does it?" asked Reece with interest. "Dingoes are Aboriginals' dogs, they tell me."

"That's right," returned Harrison with relief, very glad to learn that Reece knew nothing at at all about dingoes. With a few deft questions during the conversation, he ascertained that neither Reece nor his wife knew anything about dogs, though they had once owned a retriever that had died. Its kennel was to be Warrigal's home during his town holiday.

The meal over, the two men returned to the yard, where Reece was introduced to Warrigal. The big red and white dog came out from under the cart and fawned on his master's boots, but when Reece bent down to pat him, the dingo shrank back with bared fangs.

"A bit savage, isn't he?" said Reece, hastily withdrawing his hand.

"Actually, he isn't," said Harrison. "The fact is, he has not had many dealings with people. I've kept him away from the towns. He is a proper bush dog. Leave it until the morning and I'll introduce you properly."

"Better put him in the kennel," said Reece. "Darky's old collar and chain are still there. I'll unharness the horse for you."

With some old bags under his arm, Harrison led the dog to the kennel. He made a bed inside with the bags and then secured Warrigal with the rusty chain.

While he was making the dog comfortable, Reece backed the cart into the shed and began to unharness the horse. Harrison joined him and the job was soon completed.

"You go back to the house, Charlie," said , Reece. "I'll take the horse across the lane and let him go in the paddock. He'll be as safe as houses there."

Harrison did not return to the house. He went to the kennel and called softly to Warrigal, who came out of the kennel, whining gently.

"I guess it is going to be a bit lonesome and strange for you at first," said the bushman, patting the dog's head. "You'll get used to it and it is for your own good. You'll be a well educated dog by the time we get back to your own country. Now I'll get you something to eat, and then you can bed down for the night. Be a good dog, Warrigal. I'll see you shortly with that feed."

Entering the house, he begged some scraps from his sister, who responded generously with some pieces of meat and bread, which the bushman carried back to the kennel. Warrigal was pleased to get that meal. He was in a strange place, and already yearning for the bush, but that did not affect his appetite.

Leaving the dog to eat his dinner in peace, Harrison went to the back gate to look for Reece, who was just crossing the lane. Chatting animatedly, they went into the house where they settled down for a long chat, that lasted far into the night.

Out in the kennel, Warrigal was restless, lonely and very unhappy. He lay in the kennel for a while and then emerged, to stand and survey his unfamiliar surroundings. The yard might be strange and unfamiliar, but those glittering sky diamonds above him were all too familiar. Back went his thoughts over the many miles he had traveiled to this wretched place—back to the wide open spaces, the plains, the creeks, the bush and the ranges where he was born.

In his unhappiness, the dingo pointed his nose at that star-spangled sky, yelped a couple of times and then gave a long howl that rang into the still night like a lost soul wailing in sore distress. Lowering his head, he raised it again, and for a second time sent out his howl, as if in heart-rending appeal to the Dingo God to release him from his present bondage and return him to his beloved hills.

As the echoes of the second howl died away, minor pandemonium broke loose. In near and distant fowlyards, roosters began to crow, and in near and distant backyards, dogs of all kinds commenced barking and whining.

Charlie Harrison, deep in sleep, was dreaming of the dingo country. Once again he was walking through the hills and down the gullies, inspecting his traps. He had one set at the side of a wallaby pad that led down from the range, and when he came to it he found a big dingo caught by the hind leg.

With his gun ready, he advanced to the trap and as he raised the gun to shoot the dingo, the wild dog pointed its nose straight at him and howled in agony. It was an awful howl, the worst he had ever heard, and it nearly deafened him. He sighted the gun and was about to pull the trigger, when suddenly the dingo changed into Warrigal and gave another and yet louder howl.

At this point Charlie Harrison woke up, the howl still

ringing in his ears. The room was in darkness and as he lay there, the sound of barking dogs and crowing roosters assailed him.

"What's going on outside, I wonder?" he muttered as he sat up in bed. "I'll bet Warrigal is at the bottom of it, whatever it is."

Reaching out a hand he found a box of matches and lighted the table lamp. The clock on the shelf told him it was after one o'clock in the morning. Apparently the row outside had not disturbed the rest of the household, so Harrison quietly left his bed and, pulling on his boots, crept from his room, down the passage, and out the back door into the yard, making straight for the kennel in the corner.

It was empty, and there was no sign of Warrigal.

By the light of matches, the bushman saw that the chain was still attached to the kennel, but the other end had only a portion of leather collar hanging to it. A close examination showed him that the leather was old and weather-beaten. He had not taken much notice of it when he had tied Warrigal up, but now realised that it had not been used since the death of Reece's retriever. But where had Warrigal gone?

Back to the house he went, creeping silently to his room without waking his sister or her husband. Swiftly he dressed, blew out the lamp, and let himself out the back door again. First he went to the kennel where he collected the chain, and then to the cart in the shed where he secured a stout leather strap. Slipping the chain and the strap into his pocket, he made for the back gate and entered the lane.

Somewhere in the night was Warrigal, and he had to be found.

CHAPTER VII.

A KILLER ROAMS THE NIGHT.

WARRIGAL, listening to the barks and howls of his domesticated kinsmen, felt a strange exhiliaration, and an urge to join them. He walked up and down uneasily and tugged at his chain. It held fast, and he retired to the kennel, only to emerge again. He gave a few short yelps, paced up and down outside like an animal distrait, and then ran into the kennel again. Here he stayed for a few moments gnawing ineffectually at the chain and growling to himself.

Suddenly he heard a dog barking quite near. Dropping the chain from his mouth, he rushed from the kennel with a force that broke the perished leather collar. He was free!

With a rush, he made for the fence and went over it in a lithe scramble. In the lane he could see no sign of the dog that had barked, so he stood still for a few undecided seconds. Then he began to prowl stealthily up the narrow thoroughfare towards the main street, keeping in the shadow of the fence.

Near the mouth of the lane he saw something sneaking across the opening. It was a cat, but Warrigal did not know that. It reminded him vaguely of a rabbit, but he had never seen a rabbit with a tail like this animal. Also, all the rabbits he had known had hopped along, not sneaked.

The cat vanished, and the dingo padded softly round the corner after it, still part of the shadows. Once the cat stopped and glanced idly behind it, but did not see Warrigal, who had frozen into immobility. Satisfied, the cat trotted away up the footpath, while the dingo slid swiftly along the fence after it without a sound. The cat, a big tom, turned into another street. When he reached the corner, Warrigal shoved a cautious head round it and saw the cat trotting along. He went round the corner in a flash, stalking it silently.

The big black cat did not suspect the dingo's presence. It was wise in the ways of all domesticated dogs and knew how to deal with them. Had it known a dog was behind it, it would have flown over the nearest fence, or darted across the street and up the handiest drainpipe. But that cat had never before been stalked by a native dog.

Warrigal got to within leaping distance of the cat without the feline being aware of his existence, and, without stopping to crouch, hurled himself straight at it, his huge paws knocking the black animal flat.

Though surprised and hurt, the cat was by no means stricken. In an instant it became a scratching, spitting and fighting fury. The fact that it had been trotting along when attacked, saved it from death because, when Warrigal jumped, he intended to seize it in his powerful jaws. The pace of the cat, however, upset his calculations and, instead of his teeth meeting in its neck, only his paws struck it.

The tom cat had met and fought dogs before, and was not afraid of this one. Warrigal, expecting to have only a rabbit-like creature to deal with—rabbits never fought back, but just died—was astounded when the cat spat in his face and followed that up by sharply ripping his nose with a flashing paw. He gave back a little and the cat, its black back arched, squealed at him and showed all its teeth.

Stealthily, Warrigal began to circle round it, the cat wheeling as he did so, sharp claws ready to repel any attack.

There was a loud noise, and down the street, its headlights glaring, came a motor car. Warrigal, who had never seen a car before, took his eyes off the cat to look at this terrible monster. The cat, an opportunist, sprang at the fence and disappeared from view, while Warrigal, his own belligerence gone, melted into the shadows at the bottom of the fence and stayed crouched there until the raging, roaring, brilliant-eyed monster had vanished.

When the coast was clear again, he slid along the fence until he came to a corner. He hesitated for a moment before crossing the road, but the absolute stillness of the early morning induced him to take his courage in both paws and cross. A wide open space with trees and bushes, the park, attracted him, and he flashed into a flower bed and hid under a low bush, from which vantage point he could survey the neighbourhood.

A few yards away stretched a white concrete path, and Warrigal got a surprise when a queer object came along it. He could not, for the life of him, make even a wild guess at what it could be. He saw that it was a human being, but instead of the queer long legs possessed by these creatures, this thing had supports that went round and round. He had seen them on a cart, but never on a man.

Warrigal flattened himself into the soft earth of the flower bed, his nose half-buried, and the human law-breaker, who was riding his bicycle without a light on the footway of a public park, never guessed that he was furnishing wide-eyed interest for a dingo dog.

The dingo dog stayed under the bush for some time after the man had gone, and then the silence encouraged him to emerge from the flower garden. He flashed across the park grass like a red and white phantom and eventually came to an enclosure of wire netting.

That enclosure, or rather its occupants, made Warrigal feel almost at home, for, looking through the wire mesh, he saw several kangaroos and wallabies of various sizes. It called for closer investigation. During his rabbiting days with his master, he had had the pleasure of killing one or two such creatures as these, and he had liked the portions Harrison had allotted him.

Round the enclosure he stalked, seeking an entrance. There was none, so he would have to make one. With his powerful paws he began to dig away the earth at the bottom of the wire, and when he had made a fairly large hole, he crawled into it and succeeded in forcing up the netting by arching his powerful back. There were six or seven marsupials in the yard and, selecting a small joey not long out of its mother's pouch for good, the red and white dog commenced to stalk it. It was feeding quite close to a tree about four yards from the fence. Warrigal slipped along the inside of the wire and gained the tree trunk without any of the feeding kangaroos apparently seeing him.

With the trunk of the tree between him and the joey, he peered cautiously round it. The joey was not within springing distance, so the dingo had to take action. He waited until the joey turned its back to the tree and then he went to earth, crawling silently round the trunk, his body flattened to the ground. A big kangaroo was close to the victim, but all the others were some distance away.

With a lithe spring, Warrigal was on the young kangaroo, his powerful jaws seizing the terrified animal by the scruff of the neck and his sharp teeth literally meeting in the soft flesh. Down went the kicking and struggling young 'roo, while the big one that had been feeding near it, hopped madly away.

Warrigal wasted no time over that joey. It was quite powerless in his grip, and gave up its life with the minimum of trouble. With primitive savagery, his domestication falling from him like bark from a gum tree in autumn, he tore at the still palpitating carcase and ripped lumps of flesh from it, making a satisfying meal.

He left the enclosure the way he had entered it, the remains of the young kangaroo a mute testimony to his reversion to type. It was instinct, not knowledge, that took him through a broken fence into a yard where another wire netting enclosure penned in a number of fowls. He entered that enclosure in exactly the same manner as he had entered the kangaroo yard, and sneaked into the open fowl house.

Warrigal pulled five fowls from their perches and bit them to death without disturbing the others and was reaching for a sixth when a rattling chain and a barking dog sent him out of the yard and into the street again. He had no valid reason for killing those fowls. He was not hungry.

Back in the park again, he was contemplating a return to the kangaroo yard for another meal off the slaughtered joey, or perhaps an unprovoked assault on another kangaroo, when he sighted a lean grey cat. It was creeping along the top of a fence and as he watched, it jumped to the ground and began to trot in his direction. A handy clump of hydrangeas provided him with stalking cover and he slid beneath the broad leaves, to lie crouched to earth as the unsuspecting cat trotted up.

His experience of the ferocity exhibited by the black cat earlier in the night, taught the wild dog caution. This time there would be no miscalculation, no under-estimation of either the distance or the cat's fighting prowess.

The grey cat trotted peacefully past the hydrangeas and the dingo flew at it, seized it by the neck and commenced to worry it to death. The cat fought back as best it could, but that first horrible bite had been fatal to it.

With the blood-lust full upon him, Warrigal bit and bit and was still biting when he felt a stinging blow on the back, followed by several more, and heard a well-known voice.

"So this is what you have been up to, you dingo villain! Let that cat go, or I'll flay the living hide off you!"

Charlie Harrison had caught up with his errant pet, and that errant pet was not feeling in the least domesticated just then. The blows with the strap had hurt him a trifle, and had it been anyone other than his owner, he might have turned on that person with savage fangs.

With the dead cat under his paws, Warrigal looked down at it and then up at his master, who swore at him.

"What in the name of heaven have you been up to since you left that kennel?" the bushman demanded as he shoved the strap round the dingo's neck for a collar, and attached the chain to it. "I only hope that this cat is your only victim. Come on now, home you go, and if you don't behave yourself, I'll turn you into a scalp and make money out of you."

Warrigal trotted along easily at his master's side, feeling rather pleased with himself. Harrison, however, was a prey to uneasy thoughts. He hoped devoutly that the dog had not been on a killing bout around the town, and tried to console himself with the thought that, since puppy-hood, Warrigal had been kept away from his natural haunts and trained to forget them. There was no reason why he should go out and kill things for food, because he always got more than enough to eat; and there was no reason why he should go out and kill from pure wickedness, because that had all been trained out of him.

"I hope so, anyway," muttered the bushman, as he tied the dog up at the kennel and made sure that both the chain and strap were strong enough to hold him.

Dawn was breaking when Harrison climbed back into bed. He intended to say nothing to his sister or her husband about the night's adventures. If Warrigal had been playing up around the town, Reece would hear about it at his hairdresser shop, and mention it in conversation. Over breakfast, neither Mr. or Mrs. Reece said anything about Warrigal's howling, and Harrison was relieved.

After Reece had gone to his shop, Harrison debated the best means of spending the day. He had some business to do in connection with his rabbit skins, but that would not take very long.

"I think I'll go down town and perhaps drop into Harry's shop for a yarn," he told his sister.

"You'll get plenty of talk down there," laughed Mrs. Reece. "They say that all barbers talk too much, but some of Harry's customers are world-beaters. A few of the old hands spend most of the day there having free reads of the papers and magazines, and telling tall stories."

"I've spent so much time in the bush with only Warrigal and the horse for company that I won't mind," replied Harrison grinning.

Reece waved a shaving brush in greeting as the bushman entered the shop and sat down on a form against the wall. There were several customers in the room, and they were all chatting together.

"Of course a dog did it," one man said, "and I'm game to bet that the same dog killed Sylvester's fowls."

"But dogs don't burrow under fences and kill kangaroos and eat them," said Reece, stopping shaving a customer. "Do they, Charlie?"

"What is the argument about?" inquired Harrison.

"Old Bill Hector there is the park gardener," replied Reece. "He says that last night a dog got into the kangaroo enclosure and killed a young one. Some people in the street near the park had some fowls killed too. Bill says a dog did it."

Reece broke off and, addressing his customers all together, added, "This gentleman is my brother-in-law, Charlie Harrison. He's a rabbiter, dingo-killer and bushman, and knows all about dogs. What would you say killed the kangaroo and fowls Charlie?"

"It is wonderful what dogs will do when they are hungry," replied the bushman. "I'd say a dog could have done it."

"If it wasn't so silly, I'd say it was the work of a dingo, but the only dingoes in this town are the thugs who hang around the billiard saloon," said the man in the barber's chair.

"Dingoes don't live in towns," said Harrison.

"I know all about dingoes. I've spent years as a dogger and I know how they shun human habitation."

He did not like the way the conversation was turning, but he was determined to find out as much as he could, and to get an idea of just what the town was thinking.

"I think you are wrong about dingoes not coming near towns, mate," said a customer awaiting a haircut. "Only the other day I read in the newspapers that dingoes had attacked a man at Newnes Junction, near Lithgow, and he beat them off with his oilskin coat. Another man saw a dingo within a few hundred yards of the outskirts of Lithgow. The paper said that dingo packs, some with as many as 40 animals, were roaming the mountains around Hartley and Newnes."

"I read in the papers that an old man died in his hut near a town in Queensland and when people found his body, it had been partly-eaten by dingoes," chimed in another customer.

"Some half-starved mongrel did it," said Reece. "This town is filled with them. It is a pity the police don't shoot half of them. People have lost fowls before, you know."

"What, just killed and left under their perches?" grunted the park gardener. "As for it being a dingo, that is all rot. I'm always around town and I've never seen a dingo. I've seen plenty in my time in other places, and they do not kill like that."

The rest of the men in the shop agreed with him, and Harrison sighed with relief. He was convinced that none of the men there had ever laid eyes on a dingo, but just wanted to appear knowing.

During the days that followed there were no further developments in the mystery, and Warrigal showed no disposition to break out again. In fact he was a model dog, keeping mostly to his kennel, and never making the night hideous with his hunting howls.

Things were so peaceful that Harrison decided to have a few days in the city before returning to the bush. He wished Warrigal an affectionate farewell and told him to behave himself. To Mrs. Reece he gave a word or two of warning—never to allow Warrigal off the chain in any circumstances, and always to see that he had more than enough to eat.

"I'll look after him as if he were you, or Harry," she promised, and Harrison was content, leaving on his trip with an easy mind.

CHAPTER VIII.
THE HEAD DOG IN TOWN.

THERE was no more important dog in town in his own modest opinion, than Oscar the fox terrier. Oscar was large as fox terriers go. He was white, except for a single brown patch on his fore head and a large black one in the middle of his back. His ears were stiff, but the tips leaned gently over as if tired of always being erect. He had several scars on his muzzle and a few on various parts of his body, and he was immensely proud of those scars. They were his war medals and proclaimed him for what he was—the terror of the neighborhood and the Head Dog in Town.

For Oscar, like all fox terriers, was a fighter. He loved fighting, and would sooner take on another dog than eat a square meal. He took them as they came, playing no favourites, and he had no respect for any other dog that breathed. He had been known to half-kill a small Pekinese, and a few moments later fly at the throat of a giant Saint Bernard. He won many fights and he received plenty of hidings, but he never turned tail, no matter how great were the odds against him.

Oscar was the property of a small boy, Johnny Jenkins, and when Johnny was not, as he himself regarded it, wasting his time at school, they went adventuring together. It was their habit to march around the streets and the parks until they found some other small boy accompanied by a dog. When this occurred, Oscar immediately interviewed the dog while Johnny, without any preamble, would say to the small boy. "Us two can fight you two, any day." If the other boy was willing, the fight occurred on the spot. If he wasn't Johnny invariably administered to him three punches on the arm, at the same time chanting, "Cow's blow, bull's blow, beat yer!" This was designed to make the other boy develop quickly a marked inferiority complex and send him home howling. But Johnny was unlike Oscar in that he always picked on a boy smaller than himself. He was that sort of little gentleman.

As to the two dogs, the fight occurred nine times out of ten. Oscar saw to that.

During the long hours when Johnny was at school, Oscar used to prowl the streets alone, looking for fight and generally finding it.

Slipping through the hole in the back fence near his kennel one morning, Oscar trotted round the house and in to the main street, his ears cocked and the diminutive stub he optimistically called a tail proudly rearing its one inch straight up in the air. He went up the footpath at a jerking trot, using only three legs. One back leg was lifted from the ground for no assignable reason. He didn't have a sore leg, and there wasn't a thorn in his foot. It was just blatant flashness.

On a corner he sighted an old black tom cat. It was sitting there peacefully and minding its own business. Oscar flew at that cat like an express train and sent it swearing and spitting clean over the fence into the grocer's back yard.

With a loud bark of triumph, the fox terrier proceeded

up the street and had gone about 100 yards when he sighted a pomeranian on the other side. The pomeranian was trotting along gracefully, its head in the air, its well-washed, shining black coat gleaming in the morning sunlight. It did not know what struck it. Oscar tore across the street and, without the usually accepted sidestepping and wary calculation generally observed by two dogs when they meet, just knocked the pomeranian into the muddy gutter. The pomeranian picked itself up, gave a shrill yelp, placed its shapely tail between its legs and bolted back the way it had come, its terrified yaps sounding like heavenly music in Oscar's ears. He followed slowly in its wake, wearing a most insufferable air of pride all over his battle-scarred muzzle.

Pausing outside a white fence, Oscar thrust his nose between two palings and looked benevolently at a small black and tan dog lying on a mat on the verandah. He gave a couple of low barks to attract its attention, but the dog, a sprightly young lady treated him with disdain. Oscar had often paused outside this fence and made friendly overtures to the lady, but she was not interested in him, Head Dog in Town or not. It hurt his pride, but he determined to persevere. Faint heart ne'er won fair, black or tan lady.

Along the street came a man reading a paper. Here was a chance to impress the haughty lady!

With a hop and a skip, Oscar began to run in circles around the man, patently showing off and trying to make a big fellow of himself. He threw back his head so far as to run a grave risk of dislocating his neck, and barked loudly. The man lowered the paper irritably and when Oscar gave him a sharp nip on one heel, he gave a sudden back kick, his boot colliding hard with Oscar's nose. The fox terrier stopped his antics and when the man stooped down as if to pick up a stone, turned round and bolted. As for the black and tan lady for whose special benefit the show had been staged, she deliberately turned her back on the street and lay down facing the wall. Her whole demeanor showed that she regarded the Head Dog in Town as an ill-bred upstart.

With his pride wounded, Oscar continued up the street, trotting on all four legs, but forgot the episode of the man when he saw a fowl down a side lane. He immediately gave chase, but the hen was too quick for him, slipping through a hole in the fence. Oscar did not follow her, though the hole was big enough, but continued on down the lane hoping for something to turn up—something little, for preference. A small fox terrier on a verandah saw him and, jumping to the ground, ran up and down inside the fence, barking insults and challenges. Oscar ignored his small kinsman, knowing him to be nothing but a bragger. Had the fence not been between them, or had the gate been open, he knew that that small foxie would not have been so brave. Oscar had often seen it on the streets, and it had always fled at his approach.

A wide gap between two palings in a fence near the end of the lane attracted him and he thrust an eager nose between them. He saw a yard containing several trees, a small garden and other objects, but what claimed his attention was a dog kennel in a far corner.

Wondering if he knew the occupant and if he had met him or her on the streets, Oscar gave a short bark of inquiry. There was no response, so he barked again, this time a shade imperiously. Still no response. When his third bark remained unanswered, Oscar took it as a personal insult. If that dog in that kennel did not know that it was being inquired after by the Head Dog in Town himself, then it was high time it did.

The gap between the palings was too narrow for the fox terrier to squeeze through, so he searched around for some other means of entrance. This was readily provided by a paling with a broken bottom some yards further along the fence, and Oscar deftly wriggled under it, to make a beeline for the kennel. Peering inside, he saw a large red and white dog lying asleep, and this irritated him. What right had this animal to be lying around asleep when the Head Dog in Town wanted a fight?

So Oscar gave a loud bark, followed by a spine-chilling growl—a direct invitation to the sleeping Warrigal to wake up, come outside and get a hiding.

Though half-asleep, Warrigal had heard the barks at the fence, but had not felt called upon to acknowledge them. He did not consider himself under any obligation to every stray dog that barked through fences at him; but when he heard the bark and snarl at the very door of his kennel, it was a different matter.

He raised his head and looked at Oscar, whose hair was bristling and whose fangs were bared. He seemed all eyes and teeth and skite, so after a few seconds of mild scrutiny, the dingo yawned deliberately and stretched out again, dismissing Oscar from his mind. This was too much for a dog as conceited as the fox terrier. He gave another snarl and then, thrusting his head into the kennel, nipped Warrigal on the leg.

With rattling chain, but without undue haste, the dingo rose to his feet, magnificent in his bearing, his sharp ears erect, his body radiating quiet menace. Oscar felt slightly taken aback, but had no intention of passing up a fight. He stepped back several paces to allow Warrigal to come out of the kennel, and then flew at him with a savage bark.

Warrigal dropped flat on the ground and the surprised terrier landed square on his back. The dingo gave a heave, throwing Oscar sideways, and before he could regain his feet,

Warrigal had him pinned to the ground with his powerful forepaws. It was utterly maddening for Oscar, who voiced his protests loudly. From the dingo there came hardly a sound. With the terrier under his paws, he gave it a sharp nip on the flank.

Though he had Oscar completely at his mercy, Warrigal had no special desire to hurt him. He could have killed the terrier with ease, but finally released him.

The ungrateful Oscar repaid this clemency by immediately attacking. Warrigal met him willingly enough, and for a few moments it was an exciting battle, Oscar making all the noise and Warrigal inflicting most of the damage. It was slight damage, however, because, for some reason, Warrigal just could not take this fox terrier seriously. Added to that, being chained up, the red and white dog had no zest for an all-in fight.

The battle ended when Warrigal, seizing the terrier's right ear, neatly, but contemptuously, bit half an inch off the tip. Outraged and insulted, Oscar withdrew from the contest and made for the hole in the fence. Once outside, he thrust his head back under the broken paling and barked several most insulting remarks at Warrigal. The red and white dog yawned deeply and retired into his kennel.

Smarting under the indignities that had been heaped upon him, Oscar bolted up towards the street. It was most unfortunate for the small fox terrier that had challenged him on the way down that the front gate of its house was now open, for Oscar went straight through the gate and on to the verandah where the smaller dog was sitting on the doormat. It sprang up as Oscar flew up the steps, but it could not escape. The infuriated Oscar set upon it and in a few seconds the air was filled with barks, yelps and howls as the two terriers fought.

Suddenly the front door opened and a woman with a broom came out. She set to work impartially upon the fighting pair and got them apart after each had taken a fair share of the whacks. The smaller dog whizzed round the side of the house and crawled under it, while Oscar fled through the gate and up the lane into the main street as fast as his legs could take him.

As he made his way homewards, he told himself ruefully that it had been a rotten day—he had been ignored by a lady dog, kicked by a man, had his ear bitten by another dog, and had been belted with a broom. It had been a soul-searing experience for the Head Dog in Town.

The indignation of his juvenile owner knew no bounds when he came home from school and found Oscar minus the tip of one ear. Filled with rage, he demanded loudly to know who or what had done this awful thing. Oscar, of course, couldn't tell him, so he determined to find out by some other means.

"Come on, Oscar," he said, "we are going out to find who did it. I suppose you got it in a fight, and of course I know you belted the life out of the dog that did it, but that is not the point. I only hope that a dog belonging to a boy did it, because I'm going to bite that boy's ear off to make up for it."

Oscar did not have much inclination to go looking for fight just then, but his master's voice was imperative, so together they marched up the street, crossed it and entered the park. On the oval some boys were playing, but no dogs were with them. Scorning a shouted invitation from a school mate to join him on the swings, Johnny kept on going, Oscar at his heels. Small boys with dogs gave them a wide berth. Most dog-owning children knew of the peculiar double-challenge of Johnny and Oscar Jenkins.

Having closely prospected the park and its surroundings without finding a clue, Johnny circled round some back streets and eventually found himself in the main street again. He was crossing the entrance to a lane when Oscar darted in front of him and sped down it at full speed.

"Hey, Oscar, come back here!" shouted the boy, but the dog kept on going.

"Dash him," muttered Johnny, and turned into the lane. As he marched down it, he saw his pet stop outside a high fence, thrust his nose between two palings and then set up a furious barking. He kept this up until his young master reached him.

"What's going on here?" demanded the boy, peering through the fence. He could see nothing to excite Oscar, but the terrier was barking rude remarks at something. Then Johnny saw the dog kennel in the far corner.

"Do you know some dog here, Oscar?" he asked. "By jingo, I wonder if that kennel contains the dog that bit your ear? I've a good mind to hop the fence and have a look. There doesn't seem to be anyone at home. I wonder who lives here?"

He did not have to jump the fence to investigate the kennel, for Warrigal, annoyed by the persistent barking, emerged into the daylight and glared at the fence. He recognised the fox terrier's voice. This terrier was becoming a nuisance, Warrigal told himself. It would have to be dealt with severely. No more soft-hearted clemency.

"Gosh, Oscar," said the boy, his experienced eye taking in the details of the big red and white dog. "Don't tell me you took on that beauty!"

Oscar could have entered the yard and given his master a demonstration, for the hole in the fence was nearby. The sagacious fox terrier, however, elected to ignore that opportunity and continued to lash himself into a fury behind the safety of the fence.

"That's a new sort of dog to me, Oscar," said Johnny to his pet. "It looks like a big cattle dog, but it's got an Alsatian's ears and a Collie dog's tail. It's a cross bred mongrel of some sort."

Stooping down, he patted his terrier and urged it to come away.

"You won't do much good here," he said. "Wait until we can meet him on the street. If you can't give him a hiding then, I'll be able to help you with a few stones or with my catapult".

Johnny Jenkins was a boy like that, and the thought of stones sent him looking around for some. He found a chunk of road metal, and while Oscar kept up his barks and snarls, his young master tossed the stone at Warrigal, hitting him on the side. The dingo's eyes blazed and he gave a savage snarl. He pulled the full length of his chain, and had it not restrained him, Johnny and Oscar might have regretted the stone throwing.

Encouraged by the knowledge that the red and white dog was unable to get loose, the boy picked up another stone and threw it, this time striking the kennel with a loud noise. Warrigal growled and tugged at his chain, and at that moment Mrs. Reece opened the back door. She realised in a moment what was going on.

"What do you think you are doing?" she shouted at Johnny. "Go away, you wretched boy, and get your noisy barking mongrel out of here. If you don't stop throwing stones at our dog, I'll come over there and pull your ear for you. Do you here me?"

"I can hear you all right, missus. I'm not up on the mountains," shouted Johnny, who was no gentleman. "Come on

Oscar, let's get out of this."

Calling to his terrier, Johnny made tracks up the lane. At the top of the street, the boy turned for a parting insult:

"I wouldn't own that dog for a thousand pounds, missus," he bawled. "He's only a mongrel."

Taking to his heels, and with Oscar racing ahead, young Master Jenkins did not stop running until he was well down the main street.

Back at the house, Mrs. Reece was making soothing noises at the ruffled Warrigal and succeeded in calming him down with the help of a juicy bone from the meat safe on the verandah.

Warrigal retired to his kennel, and though he concentrated his attention on the bone, he had not forgotten the episode of the barking terrier and the boy who threw stones.

Charlie Harrison had now been away nearly a week, and Warrigal was missing him a great deal. Mrs. Reece noticed it, and mentioned it to her husband.

"He just lies in his kennel and mopes. I am sure he is fretting for Charlie," she said.

"Why not let him off the chain to run around a bit?" Reece suggested. "Let him go out and meet other dogs. It will do him no good, always being tied up. You must remember he is a bush dog and not used to the chain like a town animal".

"No, Harry," said his wife, "Charlie told me to keep him on the chain all the time. Charlie owns him and should know what is best".

Reece shook his head doubtfully.

"I'm no authority on dogs, I'll admit, but I do think Warrigal would be happier for a run round the yard now and then. There is no need to let him out into the street".

"Charlie said I was to keep him chained up all the time," repeated Mrs. Reece, and her husband let the subject drop. But that night after tea when he took Warrigal's own meal to the kennel, the melancholy look in the wild dog's eyes struck a sympathetic chord in Reece's heart. Glancing towards the house to make certain that his wife did not see him, he slipped the collar off the dingo and patted him on the head.

"Have a good old run round the yard, Warrigal. You won't do any harm, and the wife won't know. You need a bit of exercise. I'll tie you up in the morning. Goodnight, old chap," said Reece affectionately, and returned to the house.

He was out very early next morning before breakfast. Warrigal was lying asleep in his kennel and merely yawned sleepily when Reece replaced the collar and gave him a pat on the head.

"Did you stretch your paws all right last night, Warrigal?" he said, but the dingo had already gone to sleep again.

CHAPTER IX.

THE KILLER STRIKES AGAIN.

OLD Mr. Hector was filled with indignation as he glared down at the dead body of the kangaroo. It was lying in a corner of the park enclosure, and was not a pretty sight. Its throat had been torn out and there were large wounds on various parts of its body. A hole under the fence with the wire pressed up told him how the killer had gained entry.

This was a matter for the police, so off he went, breathing fire and slaughter against the mysterious killer. As he crossed the park, he met a small boy with a fox terrier, and stopped short.

"Where were you and that dog last night?" he growled.

"Chasing rainbows," retorted Johnny Jenkins who, as has been recorded before, was no gentleman. Neither was his dog, which barked at the old gardener and tried to bite his heels.

"I don't want any cheek from you, my lad," exclaimed old Mr. Hector, kicking the dog away. "You and that fox terrier of yours are the curse of this town. Did you go and sool him on to my kangaroos last night?"

"No, I didn't," replied the boy, cheekily. "Anyway, he's a foxie, not a kangaroo dog. Has something been killing your 'roos again?"

"Yes, and I'm off to the police station. You had better start thinking up a good story, my lad, because that dog of yours has been in plenty of trouble before."

"I suppose you think that Oscar killed those two sheep over in Carson's paddock, too?" snorted Johnny.

"What two sheep?"

"Somebody killed Carson's two sheep last night, and it wasn't Oscar and me. No sir! Come on boy," he added, whistling shrilly, "We can't stand here all day talking to this old goat."

"Old w-what? Did you call me an old goat?" yelled Mr. Hector and, moving with a celerity remarkable for one of his age, leaped forward and gave the cheeky boy a hearty clout over the ear. "That will teach you better manners. I'll go and see your father after I've been to the police."

With his ear ringing like a fire bell, young Johnny Jenkins took to his heels. Oscar, who had been scratching plants out of a garden plot, rushed after him, and the pair disappeared down the street.

The following week was one of intense excitement in the town. Almost every morning some fresh outrage was reported to the police, and some strange stories, most of them invented, were told. A few dead fowls in a poultry run were magnified into hundreds, a murdered cat on a corner became half a dozen at every intersection, a dead sheep was multiplied into a whole flock.

But there were plenty of authentic cases, and it was quite apparent that some killer animal was at large. The police, and men armed with guns, patrolled the town at night, but they saw nothing. When they were in one part of the town, the killer was striking in the opposite quarter. Though Oscar the fox terrier had an awful name in town, nobody really thought that he was responsible. He could kill a cat and had done so, but sheep and kangaroos were beyond his capabilities.

Discussing the problem with Constable Smith, Sergeant Brown confessed that it was something new in his experience.

"I've known dogs go berserk and do some killing, but not on a scale such as this," he said. "It has been my experience that such dogs have left traces and eventually have been caught, but this one must be a ghost. He never takes anything away with him as far as I can discover. He kills and eats on the spot, or just kills."

Strangely enough, Harry Reece, in whose saloon the mystery was a deep source of gossip, never connected Warrigal with the matter. His little artifice of letting the dog off the chain at dusk each evening and tying him up early next morning, never entered his head. To him, Warrigal was a tame and moping dog, with hardly any life in him. The only occasion he had seen Warrigal exhibit some spirit was when a small boy with a fox terrier dog had thrown stones at him. Reece had seen the episode, and his wife had told him that she, too, had seen the same boy and dog throw stones on an earlier occasion.

So Reece joined freely in the discussions at his shop, advancing theories and scoffing at those put forward by his customers. One of them insisted that a killer dingo was at large, and quoted many instances he had read of the depredations of these lone animals. The stories tallied somewhat with the happenings in town, but, as another customer pointed out, who ever heard of a lone killer dingo in a large town?

"It wouldn't last a day," said one man.

"Where would it live? This town isn't as large as all that. The majority of the dogs are known, especially those Alsatians of Kennedy's. I wouldn't be surprised if they knew something about it." And so the talk went on, but the mystery was not solved.

Charlie Harrison's stay in the city, which was to have been a few days, had now lengthened into almost a fortnight. He wrote a letter to his sister telling her how much he was enjoying the excitement of the city after the loneliness of the bush, but added that he would not be sorry to get back to the wide open spaces. He expected to return at the end of the week.

Harry Reece was correct in supposing that Warrigal was missing his master. The big red and white dog missed Harrison a great deal; and he missed also, the wild life of the plains and mountains. His nightly depredations around the town were the only outlet he had for his feelings. He did not prey on the town's poultry in sheer desperation or just to raise his spirits which were low because of his master's absence; he was following his wild instincts. The gentle leavening passed on to him by his collie ancestor was upmost during the daylight hours, but at night, was not strong enough to overcome the primitive dingo in him.

It was late at night that Johnny Jenkins, returning home from the picture show, was crossing the mouth of the lane that led down to the rear of the Reece home, when he received a shock.

Oscar had accompanied him to the theatre, but had been prevented from seeing the show by a hard-hearted doorkeeper. He hung around outside, whiling away the time by fighting any stray dogs that happened along, and when the show ended, accompanied his young master home.

He crossed the mouth of the lane a few yards ahead of Johnny, trotting along importantly, and had just reached the gutter on the other side, when he was knocked flying, by something that hurled itself from the dark lane. Johnny rushed up to discover his pet in combat with the big red and white dog at which he had often thrown stones over Reece's fence.

As he ran round the whirling, biting and noisy pair, it penetrated Johnny's head that Oscar was making most of the noise. The other dog was biting and tearing, but the only sound that came from his throat was a soft, menacing growl. That Oscar was getting the worst of the fight was apparent, and his young master did not know how to help him. He tried kicking at the struggling pair, but his foot landed on Oscar as much as on Warrigal. Then he recalled his trusty catapult, which he invariably carried in his pocket, even to the picture theatre. On more than one occasion Johnny had been ejected from that theatre for firing peanuts at the screen during a cowboy picture.

Whipping the weapon from his pocket, the lad picked up a large pebble, fitted it in the pouch and fired it. Warrigal was on top of Oscar and the stone struck him a sharp blow on the back, wrenching from him a sharp, agonised yelp. He ceased biting the fox terrier, which leaped up from the footpath and scuttled off down the road, a mass of minor wounds, and all the desire to fight knocked out of him for once.

Warrigal glared round at young Johnny, half-minded to attack him, but his back pained him too much. He ran across the road to the opposite footpath, still yelping a little. The blow on the back had been severe.

As the boy watched him, Warrigal sat down on the footpath and, lifting his head, let out a long and mournful howl that scared the wits out of Johnny. And as the dingo ran round the corner towards the park, the boy fled down the road towards his home, loudly whistling to Oscar to come back and keep him company. Oscar, however, was already in his kennel licking his wounds and feeling very sorry for himself.

CHAPTER X.

JOHNNY JENKINS WORKS IT OUT.

JOHNNY was a most unhappy boy over Oscar's downfall. It was the first time he had ever known his pet to turn tail and withdraw from a fight. The only bright spot about it was that nobody other than he had witnessed the affair. None of his school mates could point the finger of scorn at the fox terrier and say that he was no longer the Head Dog in Town. Against that, however, was the fact that Johnny himself knew it, and he found poor consolation in the knowledge that it was a secret between him and Oscar—and the big red and white dog.

It was, therefore, in no good mood that he went to school next morning. He had two fights before school went in, and his horrified mistress instructed him to stay in for an hour after school that afternoon and write an essay on Australian wild life. She selected that subject because she knew Johnny was ignorant of it. It would make him use his brains a little, and make him regret his most unseemly behaviour in the playground.

So, when the other children departed for home at the end of the day, some of them making rude faces and ruder remarks at the hapless detainee, the mistress instructed him to get on with the essay.

"I shall not disturb you," she told him. "I shall be in my office and when you have completed, say, four pages about our birds and animals, bring the essay to me, and you may then go home."

Left alone in the deserted class room, Johnny made several half-hearted attempts to scrawl a few lines, but soon gave it up as a bad job. He sat and brooded intensely on the injustice of the world in general, and of school mistresses in particular. Gradually the hands of the clock stole round, and his school book was still a blank. He knew nothing about nature study, except that it had something to do with birds and animals. He felt tempted to write a graphic description of all the fights his dog had won, but reluctantly gave up that idea. Miss Grey wouldn't be likely to accept it as an essay on wild life, though Oscar was wild enough.

Restlessly he got up from his desk and wandered over to the window. He could not see the street, but he knew that the fox terrier would be patiently awaiting him at the gate. On the way back to his seat, his eye caught the bookcase in the corner, and a dishonest idea flashed into his brain. He would copy his essay from one of those boring volumes that the mistress kept there.

Carefully sliding back the glass door of the bookcase, he ran an eye over the titles on the shelf. There were several that might suit him, especially one about animals. He was not interested in birds, except as targets for his catapult.

Returning to his desk with the book, he opened the pages at random. Kangaroos? Yes, he could take some paragraphs about kangaroos. Platypus? Yes, some of that; also a bit about koalas and possums. Then, without troubling to alter one word in the printed text, the dishonest boy began to copy whole passages as fast as he could write. He quickly filled a couple of pages. Surely that would be enough? No, she had asked for four pages dash it!

Moodily he turned the pages and came across another animal. The dingo. Yes, a few bits about dingoes would go well in the essay.

But as the boy began to write from the book, his interest became aroused. He threw down his pen and gave himself up wholly to reading.

"Dingo or Warrigal... the Australian wild dog," he mumbled aloud. "It has a sharp muzzle, ears short and erect . . . bushy tail . . . color varies between light reddish brown and black... unable to bark, but yelps . . . at night howls dismally . . . a silent hunter . . ."

As Johnny read on, his interest grew, and when he reached the end of the article, his excitement was almost uncontrollable. Forgetting his essay, his teacher and the classroom itself, he picked up the book and rushed outside. Oscar greeted him with joyful, welcoming barks, but the excited lad ignored him, and raced up the street as fast as he could go, to tear into the Police Station like a juvenile tornado.

"Mr. Brown," he panted to the sergeant, who was writing at his desk, "I know the dog that has been killing all the things around the town."

The sergeant looked quizzically over his glasses. "Is that so? Have you come to confess that that Oscar dog of yours is guilty?" he asked, a humorous twinkle in his eyes.

"No it isn't Oscar, it's that dog that Mr. Reece the barber has in his back yard. It's a dingo. It is all in this school book here," said Johnny in a rush of words.

"Calm down, my boy, and tell me what this is all about," begged Sergeant Brown.

"Here, Mr. Brown, look at the book and read it for yourself," said Oscar's master, thrusting the open book under the sergeant's nose. "Look what it says about dingoes. It is a dingo that has been killing all the fowls and things, and Mr. Reece the barber owns it."

Sergeant Brown took the book and glanced at the article. Then he requested the boy to start from the beginning and tell him the whole story.

Johnny told the officer about the big red and white dog. Tactfully, he did not mention the stones he had thrown at it. He also described the attack it had made on Oscar, and how the red and white dog had fought so silently.

"He never barked or growled all the time, and after the fight was over, he went across the street yelping and howling just like the book says dingoes do. He doesn't know how to bark. He's a dingo himself," declared the boy.

"I didn't know Harry Reece owned a dog," commented the sergeant.

"It's not a dog, it's a dingo," shouted the boy. "You go up and have a look at it."

"Yes, I suppose I could have a look at it, though I wouldn't recognise a dingo if I fell over one," said the sergeant doubtfully.

"I'll come with you and show you where it lives," said Johnny eagerly. "I'd like to get my own back on it for hurting Oscar."

"Serve him right," said the unsympathetic sergeant. "It is high time that dog of yours was taken down a peg or two. As for your coming with me, I think I am quite capable of finding my own way to Mr. Reece's home. Now, you run along, Johnny, and take your dog with you. I'll keep this book for a while. And by the way, keep your mouth shut about this, because if what you say is true, I don't want the Reece's to be warned in advance."

"I won't say a word to anyone," promised the boy, and

departed.

"What do you know about dingoes, and to save you the trouble of being funny, I am not referring to human thugs," Sergeant Brown asked Constable Smith when that officer arrived at the Police Station shortly after Johnny had gone.

"I've seen them in the zoo," replied the constable. "Why do you ask?"

Sergeant Brown told him of young Johnny's visit.

"Something has got to be done about these mysterious killings, and we cannot afford to miss any chances," the sergeant went on. "I think you had better go up and have a look at that dog."

"I won't know if it is a dingo," protested the constable.

"Well, just see what you can discover. I'll leave it to you to act as you think fit," said the sergeant, and off went Constable Brown on his errand.

It was dark when he returned to the Police Station, and what information he had made Sergeant Brown thoughtful. The constable said he had seen Mrs. Reece. Mr. Reece had not reached home from his shop.

"I told her I was just checking up on all the dogs in town to see if they were registered," said Smith. "Mrs. Reece said that the dog belonged to her brother, who was away on a holiday in the city, but was expected home on Saturday night. She did not know if the animal was registered, but said she would ask her brother as soon as he got back, and would let me know at once.

"But here is the most interesting piece of information," said the constable impressively, "Her brother, Charlie Harrison, is a rabbit trapper and dingo killer by occupation and rarely comes to town. He told his sister that he got the dog in the back country. I had a look at it. Mrs. Reece says it is never allowed off the chain. She did tell me its name, too. I wrote it down on a piece of paper so that I wouldn't forget it. It is a funny name."

Constable Brown pulled an old envelope from his breast pocket. "They call it Warrigal," he said.

"Warrigal, eh?" said the sergeant with a whistle. "That is the aboriginal name for dingo! It looks suspicious, but we must be careful. We cannot accuse Reece of keeping a noxious animal unless we have proof. We will have to try to catch it in the act of killing."

"But Mrs. Reece says it is never allowed off the chain," objected Smith.

"How do we know she is telling the truth?" demanded the sergeant. . .

It was the night of the full moon. Constable Smith, patrolling the back streets of the town, was feeling bored. The streets were empty and everything was quiet. Finding himself near Reece's home, he decided to have a look over the fence to see if Warrigal was at home. He strolled down the lane and presently came to the back fence: Looking over it, he could detect no movement in the far corner where the kennel was, and was turning away when he saw the dog emerge from the kennel and stand for a moment in the bright moonlight. It was not chained up!

Quickly the constable crouched down behind the fence and, applying an eye to a crack between two palings, watched the dog's movements. Warrigal was in no hurry to go hunting. He sat on his haunches and looked solemnly at the moon. Raising his head and pointing his sharp muzzle at it he contemplated howling, and then changed his mind. Standing up, he appeared lost in thought for a second or two, and as Constable Smith stood up to get a better view over the top of the fence, Warrigal came to a sudden decision.

Rushing lightly at the fence, he scrambled up it at the

exact spot where Constable Smith was standing. Warrigal's head came over the top at the same moment as Constable Smith's. The police officer felt a soft nose jammed in his right eye, and then he was knocked sideways, his cap falling to the ground.

With an ejaculation of astonishment, he rubbed his eye and stooped to recover his cap. When he straightened up again, there was no sign of the dog. Keeping a sharp look out, he walked to the top of the lane and glanced down the street. There were no dogs of any kind in sight. He stood there for a moment and then returned to the spot where Warrigal had jumped the fence, determined to await the dog's homecoming.

At the end of an hour he had had enough of it and, venturing to the top of the lane, almost collided with Sergeant Brown.

"Oh, there you are, Smith," said the sergeant. "Come with me. I'm calling upon Harry Reece to see if that dog of his is at home."

"It isn't," said the constable, and told him what had occurred.

"That is good enough for me," said Sergeant Brown grimly. "A few minutes ago old Peter Cleary phoned the station and told me that while he was down in his back paddock not ten minutes ago, he saw a big red and white dog sneak under the post and rail fence and deliberately attack one of his calves. He said he rushed the dog with a hay batten he was carrying, and it vanished like a shadow."

"Reece's dog!" exclaimed Constable Smith.

"I think there is little doubt about that!" replied the sergeant. "Now I am going to interview Mr. Reece."

Accompanied by the constable, he entered the front gate

and knocked on the door. There was no response, so he knocked again, this time louder. Still there was no response.

"They must be out visiting," he grunted. "Never mind, we will wait for them, and there is no better place to wait than in the yard near the dog's kennel."

Together, the two officers went round the house to the yard and sat down on the grass behind the kennel. They did not know how long they would have to wait, but they intended to see it out.

Miles away, on the outskirts of the town, Warrigal, having failed in his attempt to kill the calf in Mr. Cleary's paddock, was investigating a small poultry farm. He had never visited it before, but had no trouble in gaining entry to the fowlhouse. Creeping into the ramshackle building, he quietly and efficiently tore a young pullet from the roost and as quietly and efficiently bit it to death.

And then he did something he had never done before. He picked up the dead pullet in his jaws and departed with it. Hitherto, he had killed and eaten at or near the spot, or had just killed and left his victims where they were.

Keeping in the available shadows, he headed back for his kennel. Some deviations were necessary. Once he hid under a bush to avoid a man on horseback, and on another occasion dived up a small culvert when he heard a motor car approaching. He reached the lane by jumping over a fence and crossing the paddock in which his master's horse was grazing, and then slipped along the back fence until he reached the spot he always used either to leave the Reece yard or enter it again.

Sitting behind the kennel and talking, the two policemen were keeping an eye on the fence and both saw Warrigal's head appear above it.

"Get ready," hissed the sergeant. "Here he comes and he's got something in his mouth. It looks like a dead fowl. That's all the proof we will need."

He drew his heavy revolver as Warrigal dropped lightly to the ground inside the yard and began to advance silently towards them. Both men sprang to their feet, service revolvers in hand. Warrigal saw them and stopped dead, the pullet still in his mouth. He did not know if the men were friends or foes.

Suddenly the quiet night was shattered by a loud explosion, and the dingo felt something tear along his back, causing a sharp pain. He dropped the fowl and whirled round towards the fence. As he scrambled up it, there was another earsplitting crash, and something smashed into the palings within an inch of his head. Dropping into the lane, he fled up it at top speed, not troubling to seek out the shadows. Straight up the narrow lane he flew and was within feet of the main street, when another bullet smacked the hard pavement just ahead of him, and went humming and snarling across the street, to bury itself into a telegraph post.

Across the street in the wake of the bullet, the dingo fled. He went through the park like a red and white arrow, and up the steep hill at the other side. Not pausing in his flight, he kept on going until he reached the open country beyond.

The wound to his back had been nothing, the bullet merely parting the hair and searing the skin. Had it been an inch lower, Warrigal would never have hunted another fowl.

Without turning round to see if he was being followed, the dingo kept on going, and dawn found him many miles from the town and in open grass and grazing lands.

He spent most of the day hiding under a culvert along the road that wound up into the hills about eight miles from town, and when night fell again, continued his flight. He had no idea where he was heading, but he did know one thing: he had not the slightest intention of returning to the Reece home.

Warrigal had done with human beings forever.

CHAPTER XI.

WARRIGAL GOES HOME.

IT was incongruous, Charlie Harrison told himself, but the loss of Warrigal had created an aching void in his heart. He was by profession a dingo killer, paid to hate and to exterminate the wild dogs that caused so much damage in the back country; and yet he had grown to love one of the species.

That the object of his affection was not a pure-bred dingo made it worse, because the cross-breds were far more dangerous and destructive than the wholly native dogs. His friends had been right. There was no taming a dingo, pure or half-bred. Sooner or later its natural instincts prevailed, and it reverted to its wild habits.

As he jogged along in the old spring cart, making slowly back to the dingo and rabbit lands, Harrison's thoughts kept turning to his city visit and to the serious news that had awaited him when he got back to his sister's home. There was no use reviling his brother-in-law for having allowed Warrigal off the chain against strict instructions. Reece had been thinking of the dog's welfare; but why had not Reece's own common sense told him it would have been wiser to keep the dog chained up when a mysterious killer was abroad? Of course Reece had not suspected Warrigal, but . . .

Well, Warrigal was gone. Where, Harrison did not know and neither did anyone else. The police could not tell him anything about it, in fact he had found them most unsympathetic. Their bullets might have hit the dog, wounding him fatally; he might have crawled away somewhere to die. They didn't know and they didn't care. What they did care about, however, was the fact that Harrison had brought a noxious animal into the town, and that animal had done a lot of damage.

"Prove it," Harrison had told them; but they could not prove it. They had not caught Warrigal in the act of killing and they did not know to whom the dead pullet had belonged. Nobody had come forward to claim it.

The bushman had stoutly denied that the dog was a dingo. It was an ordinary cattle dog, he had maintained, and the police could not prove otherwise.

Charlie Harrison had not lingered in the town after his return from the city. He remained only long enough to collect stores and other necessities for a long stay in the bush, and then harnessed his horse and departed, making northwards to his old camp in the dingo country.

But there had been one very bright spot in the whole sorry affair. He learned from the police that Johnny Jenkins had been responsible for putting them on the track of the mysterious killer. Johnny always the braggart, had come to the Reece home when he learned of Harrison's return from the city, and had had the impudence to tell Harrison all about it. As he drove along, the bushman recalled with grim satisfaction that Johnny Jenkins would find it uncomfortable to sit down for a few days. The bushman had a hard hand, and the seat of Johnny's pants was not of thick material. . .

Harrison calculated that it would take him a week to reach the dingo country, but he was in no hurry. He would do some rabbiting and odd jobs for station owners on the way. His time was completely his own.

While he was driving slowly and sleepily under the heat of the noonday sun, his eyes, lazily surveying the passing scenery without actually absorbing it, came to rest on a plume of brownish smoke. It was rising steadily from behind some distant tree. and he pulled the horse to a halt.

Bush fire!

His practised eye judged the distance to be at least five miles, and he thought it came from a grass paddock.

"They will need help," he told himself, and automatically swung the horse's head around. The cart left the track and went bumping across country. As he drew nearer, the pall of smoke thickened, and on topping a slight rise, he saw that the whole of the lower country appeared to be a mass of flames.

Reaching a belt of trees half a mile from the nearest point of the blaze, he stopped the cart, quickly got down and began feverishly to unharness the horse. Having tied the animal to a tree, he ran the rest of the distance on foot and, without invitation, seized a wet bag from a heap near the water cart and joined the half-dozen soot-covered, sweating men who were hard at work beating back the flames.

The fire fighters took no notice of Harrison. There was no time for greetings, neither was there any need. It was the regular and understood thing in the outback for bush fire fighting to be waged on a community basis. It was a battle they might be called upon to fight at any hour of the day or night or at almost any season of the year. Station hands never had to be told to go and fight a fire for a neighbor. When they saw smoke, they equipped themselves for the fray and went to the task. They never knew when it might be their own property.

Harrison and his companions fought their section of the fire until sundown. They battled desperately, in dust and heat and scorching, stifling smoke, their eyes aching, their tongues parched and their heads throbbing. There was no time to stop for food or drink; actually, there was none to be had.

As the sun sank down behind a dense pall of blood-tinted smoke, they felt they had the fire sufficiently in hand for them to rest.

"Glad of your help, mate," a fair-headed youngster gasped as he beat out with his hand a smouldering patch on his trouser leg.

"Glad to be of assistance," replied Harrison, throwing his partly-burned bag to the ground "How did it start, do you know?"

"Not certain," said the youngster. "Probably the same old thing—the sun focussed on a bit of glass from a broken bottle, or some fool threw down a lighted match."

"It was that old fool of a sundowner camped over among those trees by the dam," put in a burly-looking man. "He was drunk and didn't put out his fire before he left."

"I doubt it," said the young man. "These old sundowners who are always on the track know enough not to be careless with fire. It is the casual camper, the chap who knows nothing about the country and cares less, who causes all the trouble. I can't understand why people must be so careless with fire. There are bush fire warnings given continually in the papers, on the radio and by posters, but some people just do not care a hang, as long as their own property is not in danger."

"You take some of these city folk," he went on. "They go for a Sunday run in their cars, make a fire on the roadside to make a cup of tea, and then pack up their things and drive away happily. They never think of pouring water on the embers of a fire, or placing dirt over it to make sure it is out. The first bit of wind sends sparks into the bush, and next thing there is a bush fire which does thousands of pounds worth of damage."

"You can't educate some types of fools," agreed Harrison.

The fire having been got under control, Harrison said he would return to his cart and camp for the night.

Dawn revealed a blackened stretch of countryside, but the owner of the property was thankful, because the outbreak had been confined to one paddock and only a small portion of another. He expressed his gratitude to Harrison for his unsought assistance, and offered him a job.

For the rest of that summer and portion of the winter, the bushman stayed on the property, rabbiting and assisting the stockmen in the lambing season. It was early spring when he decided to move on. His next port of call was to Mr. Jacobs' station, where he sought out the old man and apologised for not returning from that visit to the township. He explained that he had received a message in the township which had called him to the city.

Old Mr. Jacobs told him that the mysterious dingo had not been sighted, so he had concluded that the animal had moved on.

Harrison stayed a few weeks on the property doing odd Jobs, and then set out at last for the dingo ranges, reaching his old camping ground a week later. It had been nearly three years since he had left the place, and over a year since he had last seen Warrigal.

The bushman by now had given the dog up for lost. He pitched his tent and stabled his horse in the old cave up the gully and after having made everything trim, settled down for the night, serenaded and then lulled to sleep by the mournful howls of hunting dingoes. He had not heard the sound for years, and it made music, though wild, savage music, in his ears.

Next morning he was up early, and spent the day going over his old round, setting traps, laying poison baits and shooting any stray rabbits that were unwise enough to get within range of his rifle.

Making back towards his camp late in the afternoon, it crossed his mind that a juicy wallaby steak would make a most attractive evening meal. These animals were to be found at times near the foot of the ranges, though mostly they clung to the denser foothills.

As he walked towards a waterhole, the favourite drinking place of all sorts of bush creatures, the thought struck Harrison that the surroundings were strangely familiar. Of course, all this country was very well known to him, but the huge rock ahead seemed to hold some special significance. He wracked his brains, without result for a moment or two, and then all at once he remembered. It was here that he had first met Warrigal the pup.

Harrison smiled and then sighed as he rounded the rock, only to tense. He had seen a movement in the bushes just ahead. Quickly he slid back behind the rock, and, peeped cautiously round it.

As he watched, he saw a wallaby leap lightly from among the bushes and pause with twitching ears. It sat bolt upright as if sensing danger was near. And danger was near—all too near for that unfortunate wallaby because, as the bushman raised his gun to fire, two lithe forms, one red and white, and the other tawny, flashed from the bushes, side by side, and hurled themselves upon the marsupial. The red and white dingo buried savage fangs into the wallaby's hide and the tawny dog seized his big tail in her teeth.

"Good heavens, Warrigal!" shouted Harrison in amazement and, carrying his rifle in his hand, rushed from behind the rock to where the two dingoes were making short work of the wallaby.

With a startled look in his direction, the tawny female dog flew into the bushes and was gone.

"Warrigal, Warrigal, you old villain!" shouted the delighted dogger, "How are you, old timer?"

At the sound of the human voice, the dingo withdrew from the carcase of the wallaby and turned towards Harrison. Its lips were curled back in a savage snarl, and it crouched down, as if to spring at him. Harrison pulled up short, and half-raised his gun.

"Here, gosh, Warrigal, don't you know me?" he queried anxiously. "Here, boy, come over to your old boss."

Warrigal, glaring at the human intruder, felt nothing but hatred. He had had his experiences with these human beings. They had captured him, taken him to a town, tied him up and made him lead an awful life in a stuffy kennel, and just because he had followed his natural instincts and done some hunting at night after the fashion of his wild ancestors, they had shot at him with guns and tried to kill him. He had succeeded in getting away from them and, after many weary weeks, during which he had had many narrow escapes from death in several guises, had been led by instinct back to the home of his fathers.

Now, when he thought that all that was behind him, along comes another human being to scare away his mate and to deprive him of his evening meal. Well, the human being was not going to get it even if it meant a fight.

Hatred blinded Warrigal to everything else. In front of him he did not see his old master, but just a human being, and he hated all the race.

Though he did not understand what was passing in the dingo's mind, Harrison saw that something was radically wrong. He retreated a few yards, keeping his gun ready, and then, dropping down on his haunches, began to talk soothingly and to make seductive noises.

And as Harrison did so, he noticed the fierce light dying slowly from the wild dog's eyes. He saw its muscles relax, and at long last, it stood up at the side of the dead wallaby, completely calm. With that lessening of tension, Harrison knew that he had won the dog over. Warrigal looking at the man, felt his primitiveness and his hatred slipping from him. Why, he knew this man! It was his old master, his old friend with whom he had spent many happy days and weeks before they had gone away to that dreadful town!

Harrison stood up and whistled, holding out his hand and rubbing his fingers together in invitation. Warrigal trotted over to him and fawned on his boots. Joyfully, the bushman bent down, patted him and then hugged him to his chest. When he stood up, the dingo frisked around him.

With a thankful heart, Harrison threw the body of the wallaby over his shoulder and, with Warrigal trotting at his heels, returned to camp. Man and dog feasted royally that evening on succulent wallaby steaks grilled over the campfire and when Harrison retired to his bunk, Warrigal was lying outside, apparently quite happy and contented.

During the night, Harrison heard a dingo howl quite near the tent, but, being more than half asleep, gave it no thought. Just Warrigal or one of his friends, he yawned.

It was with hurt surprise that, emerging from his tent at dawn, the bushman found no sign of Warrigal. He called and whistled but there was no response. And that night, as the dingoes howled their mournful chorus, he sat outside the tent far into the early morning hours, but the big red and white dog never returned.

As the days turned into weeks, the dogger went about his task of collecting dingo scalps, but the job had no appeal for him. On his daily rounds of traps and baits he was always a prey to the fear that he would find Warrigal—not a free and friendly dog, but a maddened animal caught in a trap, or a pitiful victim of a poison bait.

Sitting outside his tent on the night that the moon was full, the dogger made up his mind to leave this territory for some other hunting field. It was a very bright moonlit night, and as the bushman's eyes idly wandered round the craggy and forbidding ranges, they chanced to light upon the big rock where Warrigal's parents had called mournfully to their captured pup, years before.

Surely history was not, in part, repeating itself?

There, high up on the rock stood two shapes, one slightly smaller than the other. Harrison knew instinctively that the larger dog was Warrigal.

"Warrigal, old boy," he called softly, "it is you, isn't it?"

As if in direct reply, the dog raised its head and howled. Its companion joined in the sad cry, their duet being taken up by other wild dogs, making the mountains ring and echo with sound.

Suddenly the two dogs became mute, and as suddenly the distant members of the canine choir ceased. Warrigal and his mate stood on the rock in silence for a few moments, and then vanished.

Next morning Harrison packed up and left. It was no place for him. Seated on the cart, he pulled the horse to a halt and, turning in his seat, surveyed the age-old hills.

"Goodbye, Warrigal, old boy, and good luck to you and yours," he said.

Then, clicking his tongue to the old horse, the bushman drove slowly away.

And, high up in a cave on the side of the hill, sleeping at the side of his handsome mate and his three furry little pups, Warrigal the Warrior had neither cares nor regrets.

THE END

www.ingramcontent.com/pod-product-compliance
Lightning Source LLC
Chambersburg PA
CBHW072150020426
42334CB00018B/1939